Please renew/return this item by the last date shown.

So that your telephone call is charged at local rate,
please call the numbers as set out below:

From Area codes 01923 or 0208:	From the rest of Herts:
Renewals: 01923 471373	01438 737373
Enquiries: 01923 471333	01438 737333
Minicom: 01923 471599	01438 737599

L32b

CENTRAL RESOURCES
LIBRARY

HERTFORDSHIRE LIBRARY SERVICE

**Please return this book on or before the last
date shown or ask for it to be renewed**

L32/rev79

NOT QUITE A GENTLEMAN

I am parshial to ladies if they are nice I suppose it is my nature. I am not quite a gentleman but you would hardly notice it but can't be helped anyhow.

Mr Salteena in Daisy Ashford's
The Young Visiters

NOT QUITE
A GENTLEMAN

ROLAND CULVER

WILLIAM KIMBER · LONDON

First published in 1979 by
William Kimber & Co. Limited
Godolphin House, 22a Queen Anne's Gate,
London, SW1H 9AE

© Roland Culver, 1979
ISBN 0 7183 01072

The quotation from *The Young Visiters* by Daisy Ashford
appears by kind permission of the literary estate of Daisy
Ashford and Messrs Chatto & Windus.

Made and printed in Great Britain by
The Garden City Press Limited
Letchworth, Hertfordshire SG6 1JS

Contents

List of Illustrations

To the memory of

TERRY RATTIGAN

Lost to the theatre too early in life, a firm friend, a brilliant author with sparkling wit and infinite compassion. I had the privilege of appearing in three of his plays, several of his films and one of his television plays. What more can an actor ask of a playwright?

Prologue

None of the characters in this story is fictitious. A number of them are still living but a large proportion are dead. That is inevitable, I suppose, when a chap pushing three score years and eighteen has the temerity, vanity and optimism to sit down and start to write his strange eventful history. As a slow writer surely for him optimism must be the operative word. The odds against the fella completing this task must certainly be chalked up at Ladbroke's at around 20 to 1. After all, he is practically sans teeth. Most of his head for quite a number of years has been sans hair. His wife maintains, and I have no reason to doubt her, that he is sans hearing. He has chronic smoker's cough and if he is foolish enough to hurry upstairs he is sans breath.

How can this story, which no doubt will take him many months to write, ever be completed? Well, if any of my fans ever read these first few words, then the story will have been published and I will have beaten the bookies. If not, I will know mere oblivion.

CHAPTER I

Early Life

My first recollection of consciousness was hearing the rustle of a silk skirt as my mother walked down the corridor to the nursery to kiss me good-night. Sometimes she would be in evening dress with bare arms and shoulders and would lift me from my cot. I remember thinking how beautifully soft and white she was and how very much I loved her.

I have no very early memory of my father, as when I was little over two years he disappeared to Davos in Switzerland for many months having broken down with TB. When he arrived home, cured of his illness, I had no remembrance of him. I was now introduced to a big man, not tall, about five foot nine, but massive. He had steel-grey eyes and wore rimless glasses and through these lenses his eyes looked very large and fierce to me and when he was angry—I appeared to give him endless cause to be so—they flashed fire. My elder brother, on the other hand, had no fear of my father and was a highly satisfactory son. He was bright and quick and could do very little wrong. I don't believe he ever saw those eyes flash fire.

At that time, when I was something over three years old, our family consisted of my father, mother, an elder sister, Evelyn, elder brother, Douglas, myself, and my baby sister, Iris, who was to become one of the sweetest beings I have ever known and funny withal. We lived in the suburb of Crouch End at the edge of Highgate. It was still partially country when I was a small boy. A hundred yards down the road there were meadows with cattle grazing and a stream running through them where one could catch sticklebacks, minnows and other aquatic creatures. But, alas, the land was sold and developed and a new road, which we hated, was made. What happened to the stream, I have no idea.

Father was a director and works manager of George Culver Ltd, an optical manufacturing firm founded by my grandfather in 1851. Grandfather was really quite a remarkable man and I daresay that his life story would be more interesting than my own. However, as I am presuming to write about myself, I haven't got much space for Grandfather. Suffice it that he lived in a large house in the rich part of our little world, with four or five acres of garden looked after by three gardeners. There was a coachman and carriage and pair and, of course, several servants including a parlour-maid, a very pretty woman, who remained a faithful servant until after his death. There was, I believe, some speculation in the family as to this girl's real status!

After my grandmother had borne her lord and master five sons and five daughters, a time arrived when Grandfather was persuaded that it would be best for her health and his contentment if she were, as it were, put to grass. So he bought her a country house where she lived with three of her unmarried daughters. He did her well enough; there was a pony and trap and adequate staff for the house and garden.

Naturally we sometimes visited Grandmother and my aunts in the country. Grandfather we visited nearly every Sunday after church, where Father—much to Mother's sorrow—did not accompany us. But we would always find him with his father when we arrived at the house which was about ten minutes' walk from church.

One of the remarkable things about Grandfather I will mention. I believe he thought he was immortal. He only just missed his century. He was bowled out with pneumonia at ninety-nine and eleven months. Mother went to see him the day before he died. She reported that he looked at her without fear in his eyes but blank astonishment and whispered, 'Do you know, lovey, I think I'm going to die!'

George Culver Ltd is still a flourishing concern and I suppose it is some kind of record that in a hundred and thirty years there has never been a strike.

One trait Father found 'irritating' in his tiresome younger son was that I thought I was a comedian. Unfortunately, Mother and an aunt, who frequently visited us, laughed at my fooling but Father was not amused; he considered I was showing off and no doubt I was.

The first plays we were taken to were of course pantomimes and *Peter Pan*. I saw *Peter Pan* several times in my youth. The first Peter I saw was Pauline Chase. I thought she was smashing although I didn't understand why Peter was played by a girl. Which actor played Hook I am not quite sure about. I have an idea that it was Arthur Bourchier, a big star of those days. But I am afraid I haven't done my homework on this and I may well be wrong and mixing my memory up with the thrilling *Treasure Island* in which he played Long John Silver. Years later, when I was thoroughly stage-struck, I saw Peter played by Gladys Cooper (much more of her later) and Franklyn Dyall as Hook. I also saw Gerald du Maurier as Hook and again Henry Ainley as the villainous pirate. But these later visits to *Peter Pan* were prompted more by my interest in these great stars and their various interpretations of the characters rather than the Barrie play.

The conjuring theatre next door to The Queen's Hall, Maskelyne and Cooke's, later to become Maskelyne and Devant's, was another exciting theatre of my boyhood. I particularly remember one trick that thrilled me but frightened me somewhat; indeed I believe it gave me nightmares. Maskelyne was 'showing up' spiritualists I was told. A woman was seated in a chair stage centre, apparently put into a trance by Maskelyne, then from her side appeared a smoky substance that formed into a grotesque human shape. Then the woman talked to it until it faded away! This is somewhat vague memory of the trick as I was only about seven at the time. After the matinée Mother comforted me at Fullers in Regent Street with cream buns and charlotte russe. But clearly I had too much comfort as I was sick in the cab going home.

After some other visit to this theatre I was persuaded to perform one of my comedy acts. I had seen a conjuror pull a cloth from under a fully-laid table, leaving the crockery on the table completely undisturbed. This seemed to me a splendid trick and not, I thought, beyond my ability. The result of my effort did not even amuse the ladies. Why I chose a Saturday afternoon when Father was at home to pull the cloth from under our nursery tea-table, I cannot say. I can hear the crash now and the cries of horror from the assembled company. Father, of course, heard the racket downstairs and arrived on the scene to observe the debris. Without being told he knew at once the perpetrator of the disaster. Curiously enough, the remainder of the evening is a blank to me. I believe the shock of the moment and anticipation of Father's flashing eyes and stream of lashing scorn produced in my fearful mind a temporary amnesia. I don't even remember Mother kissing me good-night, but I am sure that she must have done so.

Another funny joke that failed to raise a laugh from Mother was as a result of journeys to the West End on the top of the horse-drawn buses. It was too blowy for Mother on top; she travelled inside. I would always rush up to get a front seat behind the driver. There were traffic jams even in those days and on these occasions the language of the frustrated drivers used to fascinate me. I fancied myself as a mimic and after becoming fairly *au fait* with the words, phrases and accents of the bus drivers I decided that an imitation of these gentlemen given at a suitable moment in the nursery would get an enormous laugh—Mother struck me! I was never allowed on the tops of buses again. I have played many comedy parts in the theatre and have sometimes failed to get laughs that I expected—but the bus drivers were the flop of my life.

The first play that I was taken to see other than *Peter Pan* was *The Scarlet Pimpernel* with Fred Terry. The Terrys were a very famous theatrical family and Fred was a real charmer with a beautiful voice. John Gielgud is a Terry on the distaff side, and his inheritance has stood him in good stead. The Pimpernel, I suppose, was Fred's most famous part, but he was very successful in many others. He nearly always played with his wife Julia Neilson. She was not, I think, as good an actress as he an actor but by no means disgraced him as one or two other actors' wives did in those days. Fred so thrilled me as Sir Percy Blakeney that after seeing the play I immediately read all the Pimpernel novels. I didn't have to imagine the hero—I knew him—I had seen and heard him quite clearly. In 1931 when I joined the Green Room Club, Fred Terry was President. I was immensely thrilled to sit down at the bridge table with him.

From 1907 for many years we mostly spent our summer holidays in the Isle of Wight. We sailed a great deal during these holidays and sometimes whilst sailing we would spin for mackerel and perhaps land twenty or more of these beautiful fish. On one occasion I contrived, in my careless manner, to sit on my cousin Eric's fish-hook. This was an exceedingly painful accident, but might have been a lot worse; I was straddling a seat and the hook only missed my genitals by an inch. Fortunately, the barb of the hook had only just got beyond the surface skin and my uncle, who was with us, cut a hole in my trousers, inspected the damage, told me to grit my teeth, then yanked out the hook. It hurt! Uncle said, 'That was a near thing, I might have turned you into a lifelong soprano.' He made himself laugh, but I didn't see the joke.

After our summer holiday of 1908, Mother took Douglas, now nearly ten, and me, aged eight, to our prep school at Cliftonville in Kent. Mother kissed us good-bye and told me to be a good boy and work hard, which I fear I never did.

Although I didn't work at my lessons, I was good at games. By the age of ten or eleven I had gained my cap for the First Eleven at soccer, where I played inside left, but could kick equally well with both feet. Hockey, which was introduced to our school later on, was another game I was happy at and again achieved the First Eleven somewhat later on in my school life. But at cricket I did not succeed in getting a better place than twelfth man. I was not at all bad in the field, but I found it extremely difficult to keep a straight bat. I suffered from an irresistible desire to hit every ball for six. I was also good at gym. This gymnastic prowess strangely diverts me on to the subject of sex. My rope climbing was particularly dexterous and when scaling the double rope, that is two ropes two feet apart, gripping them firmly with hands, feet and knees, then descending with arms outstretched, sliding gently down, I discovered it gave me a most pleasurable sensation. Not that I had a complete orgasm, I did not develop this manly status until I was over fourteen. Nevertheless, I regarded the ropes with glee and perhaps anticipated some day still greater pleasure to come (that is not an intentional vulgar play on the word). No doubt this sexual experience when rope climbing might lead a psychiatrist to suppose that it created in me a lifelong passion for ropes. But it is not so. Through my teens and early manhood I never gaped goggle-eyed at a rope with any unnatural longing. Ropes after my prep school days were things to heave on to trim a sail or chuck over an anchor or tie up to a mooring.

Whilst on the subject of sex, I was never conscious of any homosexuals in my prep school. Two masters during my time there were sacked as a result of complaints to parents by boys who had been 'interfered with', but I was quite ignorant at the time of the reason for the abrupt departure of these masters. Later, when I heard the details, I was only mildly interested. I was never 'interfered with' myself and I never had any crushes. My small collection of friends from my public school, day boys like myself, were all very conscious of the other sex. We looked out for any slightly permissive girls available; the numbers were very limited and all were virgins and remained so. Complete surrender to the natural desires being too hazardous, pleasure could be obtained without going to such dangerous lengths. Looking back I suppose it was all rather messy and unsatisfactory but better, I think, than getting a fourteen-year-old girl pregnant.

Returning to my non-sexy prep school days, I was really quite happy at this school. The food was wholesome of its kind and plenty of it. Real gastronomic satisfaction had to wait until Mother came down to stay during half-term and then we would tuck in. On one occasion when staying at her hotel I met the first actress with whom I ever fell in love. I was nine or ten, she was nineteen or twenty. She was a tall, elegant, beautiful girl named Marie Lohr. Mother, I remember, was delighted to meet her for she admired her very much. She had seen her quite recently as Lady Teazle, and as Ophelia. In the basement of this hotel there was a playroom with a badminton court. So badminton we played. There was also a piano and Marie used to play and we used to sing together. Two songs that she taught me were 'The Honeysuckle and the Bee' and 'If I Could Plant a Tiny Seed of Love in the Garden of Your Heart'—well, she did that.

I never had the pleasure of appearing in a play with Marie; indeed I never met her again until I directed a revival of *Aren't We All?* by Freddy Lonsdale at the Haymarket Theatre in 1953, in which she appeared. I reminded her then of the 'tiny seed of love' which she had sown—Dear Marie—she remembered the hotel but she had forgotten the little boy.

Naturally during my several years at my prep school I did not remain unscathed. I had one or two scraps with other boys and got into various scrapes which earned me some canings, not deeply resented as I was aware that I had deserved them. I received other lesser punishments, one of which I suffered during my last term, the summer term of 1914. This punishment had some lasting results.

One master, Mr Featherstone, who was comparatively new at the school, found in me something other than the pleasant idiot that I had previously been accepted as. It was partly by accident that he suddenly showed this interest in me. I had committed some crime, the nature of which I cannot recall. Mr Featherstone decreed that I should be kept in from swimming for the following two days. (During the summer term lessons finished in the mornings at midday and we would go to the sea until luncheon at one o'clock.) During these two mornings of restraint I was to learn two speeches from Shakespeare, Hamlet's well-known advice to the players and Henry V's rejection of Falstaff beginning, 'I know thee not, old man: Fall to thy prayers', in the last scene of *Henry IV, Part Two.*

I was anxious to avoid losing two swims if possible and easily crammed in those two speeches the first morning. After prep that evening I knocked on Mr Featherstone's study door.

'Come in,' said he.

In I went. 'Please, sir, I know them.'

'Know what? Those speeches?' he asked. 'I don't believe it. Let's hear them.'

So I reeled them off without a hitch. This approximate dialogue ensued:

'Very good, Culver, very good indeed, but it is a pity that you seem only to concentrate under duress.' 'Oh, but I enjoyed it, sir, it was easy,' I replied. 'Was it, Culver? Well, well, your punishment seems to have achieved something—discovered something you can do easily. Have you ever thought of the theatre?' 'Do you mean play in it, sir?' 'Yes, boy, as an actor.' 'Well not really, sir, but I do love the theatre.' 'You do? Well, I'll have to talk to the Headmaster and perhaps write to your parents during the holidays.' 'Oh, thank you, sir. May I swim tomorrow?' 'Your punishment was two days, wasn't it? However, you seem to have worked pretty hard, so perhaps we can forget the second day.' 'Oh thank you, sir.' 'All right, boy. Hop it. Good-night.'

Soon after this event Featherstone had good cause to forget about his intended protégé. The assassination in Sarajevo took place on 28th June and Austria-Hungary were about to declare war on Serbia. I remember Mr Featherstone in class pretty accurately describing to us the inevitable result of this situation. He was a reserve officer in the British Army. He drew a map of Europe on the blackboard and showed us the possible future battlefields of that Continent. England, he said, would no doubt stand with France. In which case, he would probably arrive in France with a British Expeditionary Force and would, said he, pointing to the blackboard, he suspected, be having his Christmas dinner somewhere on the Western Front.

He may well have had his Christmas dinner on that very spot. His last. He was killed in January 1915. This I learned from a school friend who left the same term as I did. He had read of it in the casualty lists published that month.

So ended the promise of help from the only chap who might have persuaded my parents of my only possible future; perhaps then I should not have wasted so much of my youth. Certainly, paternal opposition would have been immediate at any suggestion of the theatre as a career for me. But the battle would have been fought and won sooner. As it was, it was delayed for years.

CHAPTER II

Through the First War

The summer holidays of 1914 we spent at Bournemouth, where we arrived on 2nd August. On the 4th England was at war. Nothing much happened. People started waving flags. Brave little Belgium was the hero.

After these holidays I went as a day boy to Highgate College. My Highgate days were rather few. I played soccer again. I ran in the sports mile. I played, or tried to, cricket again. I also played fives which I enjoyed enormously. But I did not work—except at English and History. After three terms of bad reports Father said no more. He said I must leave the school and have a crammer. A crammer! What a horrific word. A tutor was found locally, a grim, dour, learned man—the sort of character Dickens could have described more clearly than I. When I was seventeen Father finally accepted the fact that I was no scholar and I accompanied him to the family firm.

During the years with the tutor, Mother, who had inherited a comfortable income from her father, gave me generous pocket-money and I was able to join a tennis club, which compensated in some measure for the lack of playing fields. I had two or three friends from Highgate School with whom I would gamble at solo whist. Only one of these boys, named Alan Wilkie, is important to my story. We became good friends. He and his mother and father played a very important part in my life subsequently.

Towards the end of 1915 by brother Douglas had let my father down. At least, my father thought so. Father expected Douglas to matriculate, go on to a university and finally become an oculist.

Douglas had ideas other than swotting for matriculation, going to a university through medical training and finally sitting in Harley Street looking at eyes. He had always had a craze for aeroplanes.

What he wanted, he insisted, was to go to Grahame White's Flying School at Hendon and learn to fly. I think the battle was fierce but brief and Douglas won. Douglas always won against Father, he was far more efficiently armed than I. He left his studies at school and off to Grahame White's he went. He succeeded in gaining his pilot's certificate and at about the age of seventeen and a half became a fully qualified civilian flying instructor. At this period of the war many officers and NCO's who volunteered to be transferred from the infantry or cavalry regiments to the Royal Flying Corps were given their initial flying instruction by civilian pilots at various flying schools, such as Grahame White's, at Hendon Aerodrome.

At George Culver's I did not get on with Father better than I did at home and my work bored me as much as my school maths. This life was not what I wanted. The theatre was the only place for me. But what in the theatre? Shakespeare, which I had learned for Mr Featherstone? Or musical comedy? I could sing well enough in those days. Or a light comedy actor like Charles Hawtrey? I didn't know. I just wanted to be in the theatre. Even tragedy perhaps. I felt I could do it all. But in the winter of 1917 the war seemed as if it was going on for ever and in a few months I would be a soldier. Why have a terrible row with Father and perhaps never get near a theatrical manager before I was in khaki? No, I must wait until after the war.

I joined up as an RAF cadet at Hampstead on 31st July 1918. Cadets were only stationed in Hampstead for about four days, where we received the groundings of infantry drill up and down FitzJohn's Avenue. We then journeyed to St Leonard's for six weeks where we continued infantry drill. The only training which concerned flying was instruction in the workings of the Gnome Le Rhon aero engine and learning the Morse code. If we did not become proficient very soon at the Morse code, learn the innards of the aero engine, also be immaculate on parade, a terrible threat hung over us. We were liable to have RTU stamped on our papers, meaning Return to Unit. In other words, we were kicked out of the RAF and transferred to an infantry regiment. I was determined that was not to be my lot, so I worked harder than I had ever worked in my life.

Actually I found the parade ground the greatest hazard. This was the wide St Leonard's seafront. Here the whole wing would stand to attention, rifles at the slope, while they were inspected by the CO, one Captain Cox, who was escorted by a terrifying little Regimental Sergeant Major from the bantams. He was only about five foot five but as smart as paint with a gigantic high-pitched scream.

On parade our webbing belts had to be pipe-clayed whiter than white. The brass buckles on our belts had to shine like the sun, as did the buttons on our tunics. Our bayonets and rifles were also expected to have a high polish. Our boots should seem to be made of mock patent leather. We simply had to dazzle. Dirty fingernails seen showing as we held our rifle butts were not tolerated. This glittering entertainment was usually watched by a number of flappers who each had an eye on a chosen cadet.

As Captain Cox with the little RSM walked down the ranks, they might hesitate in fromt of some unfortunate cadet. The RSM would usually be the one to point out some blemish in the chap's appearance; he would first stare at the offending belt, boots or buttons, glance at the Captain who would nod. He would then scream, 'Cadet Blank! One pace forward, march!' Cadet clearly would obey this order. One pace would be taken, heels would click. Then the little RSM would scream: 'Cadet Blank, dirty belt, dirty boots, filthy dirty turn-out. Orderly room midday. One pace backward, march.

Apart from the unpleasant anticipation of the fatigue that Cadet Blank would be sentenced to in the orderly room later and the dressing down which doubtless he would receive from Captain Cox, there was the added mortifying embarrassment of being thus publicly reprimanded in front of all the flappers!

Of course 1918 was not exactly the permissive society that it is today; but at St Leonard's and Hastings a few permissives were to be found. One was a very pretty pink-cheeked, brown-eyed girl named Rosie; the appellation suited her very well! She was not a flapper, she was twenty-one or two. I met her in a tea-shop. She smiled. I smiled. And our acquaintance ripened. She was not in any of the women's services, presumably because she looked after an invalid aunt. She lived with this aunt in a small house in the centre of the town. The aunt never appeared, she was confined to her rooms on the first floor, being unable to walk up and down stairs. Rosie had a bedroom and sitting-room on the ground floor.

I was aware that I was not the only cadet to receive her favours; indeed a chap in my flight, Cadet Melford, whom I stood next to on parade, had also met Rosie in the same tea-shop. Rosie believed variety to be the spice of life! Clearly she got pleasure in improving our somewhat inexperienced love-making. What I did not realise was that her proclivity for passion was not confined to cadets.

One afternoon, when off duty until mess at seven, I was with Rosie in the house. She was about to draw the bedroom curtains when she stopped and exclaimed, 'God almighty! I didn't expect him today. Quick, hop it through the kitchen out of the back door and over the fence before he sees you. It's the shrimp.'

'What,' I said, 'the RSM?'

'Yes,' said Rosie, 'Hop it quick. He thinks he is the only bloody pebble on the St Leonard's beach.'

I needed no second warning! I became jet-propelled. While I shinned over the fence I prayed that he had not seen me through the window as he walked up from the gate. I thought it unlikely, but I hurried back to my billet in dreadful uncertainty and set about spitting and polishing, being determined not to give him the slightest excuse to haul me out of parade the following day. However, I need not have worried. He had not spotted me. I must admit to having had a private but somewhat disloyal chuckle at the thought that my friend Cadet Melford might be caught by the shrimp with his trousers down.

It is curious how, through life's strange history, changes occur so quickly from farce to drama. Some few days after this event, I had cause to report to the orderly room to request Captain Cox for twenty-four hours compassionate leave, as that morning I had received a sad letter from Mother telling me that my brother Douglas was missing. In 1917 he had left Grahame White's and was now a fighter pilot in France. At that time if a fighter pilot was missing it was pretty long odds against his being alive. I was granted leave to visit my parents. I think it was some comfort to Mother to have me at home for two nights. Well, Douglas was not killed. Some few weeks later I learned that he was wounded and a prisoner in Germany.

After some six weeks at St Leonard's the wing moved on to another course at Shorncliffe. From there to Denham, to the School of Aeronautics; I had just finished this course and was about to go to the School of Gunnery at Uxbridge, when an order went out on the morning of 11th November to the whole wing to leave whatever duties we might be performing and assemble in a large mess hall. Here our CO informed us that the Armistice had been signed half an hour earlier. There arose an enormous cheer and within another half an hour, without any of us receiving leave, the camp was empty. With many other chaps I walked several miles to Denham Station, where I boarded a train to London and a bus home. I had just acquired my flight cadet uniform; previously we had ordinary Tommies' uniforms with a white band around our caps. Now we wore the same new RAF uniform as an officer, except as flight cadets we had no rings of rank.

I stayed at home for, I think, two weeks, enjoying myself at theatres, mostly musical comedies and revues. One of these revues was named *Buzz Buzz* and an actor, one Walter Williams, sang the song 'Katy'. Walter Williams first sang this himself and then asked the audience to sing it with him. After this a lady was requested to do so by herself and then a gentleman was required to do a solo. I, with one or two other chaps, had dined rather well and was sitting in the stalls on this occasion. At the request for a single gentleman I got up and let myself go. That was my first effort in a West End theatre, but on the wrong side of the curtain! However, it gave me a thrill. I was still hoping to be something in the theatre but I didn't quite know what!

One day when I had been home about two weeks, I received a telegram from a pal in my flight: 'Better come back. Trouble. You are still in the Service.' Back I went to camp as quickly as I could. On arrival I was severely reprimanded and put under open arrest. Absent without leave. There were a couple of dozen of us in a similar position. What would happen? We were all very worried indeed. By now it was the end of November and bitterly cold; there was also a 'flu epidemic.

After about three days of open arrest without, as yet, any further punishment being resolved, I woke up one morning with the shivers, feeling ghastly. I woke the fellow in the next bed and asked if he would go and report me sick. It turned out that I had a severe dose of the influenza epidemic that was sweeping across the country. I learned afterwards that my temperature had been over 105. I was in bed, I think, for three weeks. I was then given two weeks' sick leave and returned home again. It was now nearing the end of December.

It was on Christmas Eve while I was still on sick leave, that my parents received a request from the Air Ministry or RAMC officials to visit them to discuss my brother Douglas. This, of course, they did at once. They were told that he was critically ill in the Anglo-American Base Hospital, run by Lady Hatfield and Elinor Glyn, at Wimereux in France. They were also advised that it would be as well if they travelled to Wimereux to see him; immediate transport would be arranged for them. They left the same evening. On arrival at the hospital they first saw the head surgeon, who was most kind. He warned them that Douglas had very little chance of living and that they would be doubtless very shocked at his appearance. He explained to them that for Douglas to have the faintest chance of surviving his left arm must be amputated at the shoulder. Douglas, when my parents last saw him in England, was a fellow of just under six feet tall and a big man, weighing about twelve stone. After the consultation with the surgeon my parents were allowed to see him; he was semi-conscious, able to recognise them, but they were practically unable to recognise him. When they talked to him and told him that he was to lose his arm that evening he was philosophical about this and said that he had been pretty certain himself that he would lose it.

Douglas's arm had been cast in plaster in Germany and they had left it at that. The pain that he suffered was intolerable and the Germans apparently could do little to relieve him. They had neither the staff nor the equipment at this stage of the war. What the Germans seemed to have plenty of was morphia and Douglas had been kept under sedation for many weeks. He never complained of his treatment in his German hospital. The Germans did not starve him—that was not the reason for his emaciation. Whatever food he was able to swallow simply passed straight through him owing to the septicaemia.

That, then, was his condition when his arm was amputated that night. He survived this operation, but very little improvement in his condition seemed to result. Indeed, his health did not seem to improve to any extent for some weeks. His spirits were desperately low; the English doctors were endeavouring to cut down sedatives, lest, should he recover, he might be addicted. The surgeon told my parents that he considered the only hope, in spite of the dangerous trials of the journey, was for him to board a hospital ship and be taken home to an English hospital. And so it happened that towards the end of January he was transported to England and arrived at the Prince of Wales Hospital in Marylebone. My parents arrived home a few days ahead of him.

Douglas continued in misery and pain for some weeks but, mercifully, began to fight off the septicaemia and gradually regained his strength. By the summer of 1919 he had been discharged from hospital, weighing around ten and a half stone.

Although being demobilised on 7th January, according to my papers transferred to Class G Reserve, I was still in uniform for most of the month. My elder sister, Evelyn, had been allowed to train to become an actress at Sir Herbert Beerbohm's Tree's Academy of Dramatic Art, later to become The Royal Academy of Dramatic Art. If Evelyn was to be an actress, why not I an actor? I would speak to Mother—but not yet. I knew it would be a declaration of war with Father. How could I create more distress for my parents after the months of worry they had had with Douglas?

I should point out that Father had no strait-laced ideas about the theatre. Evelyn was a very pretty woman and would probably get married one day. If she wished to be an actress, well and good. But actors were, I knew, a very different matter in Father's mind. I am unable to explain Father's prejudice regarding actors. As far as I am aware he had only known one actor in his life and that was a second cousin of Mother's and apparently a very respectable chap and successful. He was Courtice Pounds. I saw him in *Chu Chin Chow* in which he sang that very charming and amusing duet with a well-known soubrette Violet Essex, 'Any time's kissing time'. Nevertheless I knew pretty well the horror and rage any suggestion from me that I wished to grace the boards would cause. So I decided to postpone this request, even to Mother, for the time being.

Having temporarily given up the idea of a theatrical career, I returned to work with Father at the end of March, but not at George Culver Ltd, for Culvers, with another optical firm, had acquired a large factory built before the war by Carl Zeiss, the German lens manufacturers. A new company was formed, The United Kingdom Optical Company, with Culvers the largest shareholders at the time. Much machinery old and new was contributed by Culvers. Father designed most of the new plant.

At the time I joined the firm my first job was to assist in the assembly of the new machinery. This I found quite interesting, though I was still stage-struck, but during the next few months the idea of the theatre started to become a dream castle in the air. Particularly, I remember, when the first person to whom I confided my ambition was my elder sister Evelyn, who was by then playing leading parts on tour. She laughed me to scorn.

'Don't be so stupid, Roland. Whatever made you think that you could be an actor?'

That brief discussion somewhat deflated my ego, and clearly I was not going to get any assistance from that quarter, so I struggled on unhappily at the UKO.

I think that about the spring of 1921 I recovered from the laughing discouragement I had received from my sister and confided my discontent to my mother. I believe Mother was not surprised at my admission but she persuaded me to wait. She said something to this effect:

'Give your present job a chance. You are getting on much better with your father now. You are working in a firm with a splendid future; why throw it away for a romantic dream?'

I argued that it was not a romantic dream and I felt sure it was something that I should be able to do better than anything else I had done in my life. She pleaded with me to wait for a while.

'You are only twenty; if when you are of age, you are still determined, I will help you all I can.'

I gave in, but it meant another six months. Unfortunately as it turned out it meant another two and a half years.

CHAPTER III

Eyes of Blue

In the summer of 1921 I had not changed my mind about my career and I only had about six or seven weeks to reach the key of the door status, when I met a pair of blue eyes with lashes three inches long. Well, perhaps that is a slight exaggeration. Let's say an inch. No? All right, damn it, half an inch. Black hair, beautiful figure, lovely hands elegant legs and very white skin. My readers may have guessed that I had fallen in love!

This was an entirely new sensation. A beautiful girl who liked me, and laughed at my poor jokes. She had a delicious tinkling giggle, I remember. That sounds terrible, but I loved it at the time. She liked the things I liked, even betting on horses. Also the theatre. Indeed she was an actress. When I say an actress, so far she had only achieved the front row of the chorus and understudy. However, I didn't tell her of my wish to become an actor. I feared she might laugh the wrong way like my sister. Incidentally she too was called Evelyn. Perhaps the fact that she was in the theatre made her that much more glamorous to me. Be that as it may, I was a goner.

We met continually for the next several weeks. One day towards the end of August I hired a car and drove to Cookham, one of the loveliest reaches of the Thames. I procured a punt, every bird in the willows sang for me and I asked her, not exactly on my knees, we were lying side by side, if she would marry me! My God, she said yes. Yes, she said, just like that. Bang off, no hestitation. I couldn't believe it.

When I left her that day I walked on air. Certainly there were one or two air pockets through which I slipped. Now I had surely cooked my theatrical goose. How could I expect this girl to marry a prospective Thespian, who would, no doubt, be cut off with the proverbial shilling if I left my job? Obviously I must now abandon any hopes of the other side of the curtain and stick to my father and the factory. Sexual attraction and romance had gained priority. The air pockets were not deep enough to envelop me and my feet never really touched the ground. 'To be in love and to be wise is scarce even granted to a god.'

Well, I was certainly no god, and, as Mother pointed out when I informed her of my betrothal, I was desperately lacking in wisdom. I was far too young, she maintained, to consider marriage for at least three years. I protested at this lengthy postponement. However, Mother, with Father's strong support, was adamant. She would interview Evelyn's mother—her father had been killed in the war—and persuade her that I would be in no financial position to marry for some time.

'What,' Mother asked me, 'are you going to use for money? You have not saved a penny in your life as far as I know.'

Mother was more or less right. My bank balance behaved rather like a yo-yo according to how the horses and cards ran. So a long engagement was arranged. Of course I had made an unhappy mistake. Naturally it was not unhappy at the time, we were very much in love and for many months enjoyed a close and warm relationship. As yet Evelyn's theatrical career had only progressed to a few lines in *Pinkie and the Fairies*, and as she frequently complained to me of the difficulty of getting on in the theatre without influence it occurred to me that she would not take kindly to the idea of my chucking my safe job in Father's firm and joining her in a theatrical struggle. So in spite of my suppressed yearnings I did not confide them to her. Romance and physical attraction for the time being had won the day.

In 1922 Evelyn was in the chorus and understudying in *A to Z* at the Prince of Wales Theatre, with Jack Buchanan, Gertrude Lawrence, Maisie Gay, whose part was afterwards taken over by Bea Lillie, or maybe it was vice versa. I saw that show so many times that I knew every number by heart.

Towards the end of 1922 the prologue of the drama of my romance literally went into rehearsal.

My cousin, Eric, was a hard worker at raising money for his pet charity, St Dunstan's Home for the Blind. He telephoned me one day and said that he and a few friends were about to produce an amateur production of a farce, the proceeds to go to St Dunstan's. Would it amuse me to have a go at the leading part? Well, that was that. I think we took six weeks to rehearse this play, twice weekly. Somehow, cousin Eric had contrived to sell out the house. The venture was a financial success and the audience laughed.

Now the greasepaint had penetrated my skin and started to course through my veins, while illogical and frustrating ideas muddled my mind. After this success, Eric decided that we must put on another play, as soon as maybe. This we did.

Altogether I played in four farces or farcical comedies during the next twelve months. The first one, *The Strange Adventures of Miss Brown*, was a kind of poor man's *Charley's Aunt* and the only time in my life that I have ever appeared in drag. I remember little about it except that my character was in love with a Ward-in-Chancery who was more or less incarcerated in a girls' college and no male visitors allowed. Hence my disguise as a girl. The mere thought of it now embarrasses me. However, the audience laughed. The second play was *Facing the Music*. Again I can remember nothing of the plot. I only recall that I laughed continually—in the script—at the dreadful scrapes my friend, played by cousin Eric, got into. Incidentally, when I became a student at the RADA I won E. S. Willard's prize for spontaneous laughter! The other two plays were *A Little Bit of Fluff* and *Nothing But the Truth*. *Nothing But the Truth* was a meaningful title for me, as now the truth had to be told. I must be fair to my girl and my life. I was determined to become an actor. By this time, it was nearly the end of 1923.

Evelyn, poor darling, had seen nothing sinister in my playing in these amateur shows; she thought it rather fun and when we were together when I was learning my parts she would hold the book and hear my lines for me. So the shock to her when I told her that I must become a professional actor was profound. She just couldn't believe it. Did I suppose we could be happily married living in poverty, staying in sordid rooms whilst I trudged around theatrical agencies seeking work for which I had no professional experience? She advanced all the objections that I had anticipated. I protested that I knew I should succeed. If she really loved me she would stand by me and believe me. Poor darling girl, how could she possibly have believed in this stage-struck oaf? What did I suppose her mother would say? I had no answer to that one. There were tears and I felt that I was being an unutterable cad.

'Wait,' she begged me, 'through the winter. You will change your mind, I know you will.'

I couldn't stand this scene any longer and gave in. I promised to do nothing further with my plans until the New Year. But I warned her that I knew I would not change my mind. She said, 'I shall have to tell Mother about this, of course. I hope that you will come and see her too.'

It was a Saturday night after her show in a little private room over a restaurant in Soho where we used to sup together. After supper she was to have come back that night to our house for the weekend, but she said that she would not do so now. She thought that it would be best if she went to her home and I to mine and that I should visit her and her mother the next day.

Next morning I had Mother and Father to face. I couldn't face telling my story to both parents at once; I had to get Mother alone and tell her first. So I hedged or, to be accurate, lied. 'Evelyn's mother is not quite well so she went home. I'm going over there later.' Fortunately, it was a lovely day and Father had some job he wished to do in the garden. Mother went up to her room saying that she must change her dress, as the one she had first decided on was too hot for such a day. It is curious how certain details on such occasions remain in one's memory after so many years. I followed Mother up to her room at about ten o'clock so there was plenty of time before church to get this weight off my chest.

The whole story tumbled out. I unfolded the previous evening's scene with Evelyn. Mother regarded me with much more sorrow than anger, but promised me that it would not be the same with Father. This I was well aware of. Mother at once realised that the die was irrevocably cast and that nothing would stop me in my determination to enter the theatre. Mother said that when the time came she would help me all she could.

'Now,' said Mother, 'I think I must change and go to church. Iris will accompany me. I think it best if you face your father with the news when we have gone. I suggest you go and tell Iris about it.'

This I did. 'Oh gosh, Ro!' (Iris always called me 'Ro'. I suppose she preferred to think of me as part of a fish rather than half of a pudding!) 'Gosh, Ro, there will be a rumpus.'

So I was left to face Father. I did not normally drink anything at 10.45 in the morning but I sought a little Dutch courage in the shape of a small whisky, washed down with half a pint of beer. I then started out to Father in the garden. However, he was on his way in, so the interview took place in the drawing-room. He started with, 'Not at church with your mother?'

This was rather stating the obvious and as I was somewhat keyed up I very nearly pointed this out to him in a facetious manner—fortunately, I restrained myself.

'No, Father, I wanted to talk to you.'

'Oh really, what about?' We were standing quite close together, facing each other. He continued: 'You've been drinking, haven't you?'

'I . . . I had a glass of beer, sir.'

'Why do you want a beer at this time of the morning? You stink of drink. I suppose you had too much last night.'

This was not a promising start; however, I now plunged in the deep end. I can't recall any further part of my dialogue. That I explained my desires and intentions with a gush of verbal diarrhoea, I know, for he stopped me with—'That will do! That will do! Do you hear me?'

Did I hear him! I imagine the whole neighbourhood must have heard him.

'You bloody young idiot. You blithering, ungrateful, piddling dolt. Christ Almighty, I don't even know enough dirty names to call you! You—an actor? A fucking actor!' That is what he said, I fear. That is what he said. And continued, 'What in God's name put this stupid notion into your muddled, miserable, misguided numbskull? Just because you have appeared in a few amateur plays with that half-witted cousin of yours—poor Eric—you think you are Irving, Tree, Forbes-Robertson, Dan Leno, Fred Terry, all rolled into one. What about your girl? Have you mentioned this rubbish to her?

'Yes, I told her last night.'

'I see. So that is why she is not here for the weekend? Chucked you, eh?'

'No, I'm going over there this afternoon.'

'You don't mean to tell me that she will marry you on those terms?'

'She says not, but I hope that she will change her mind.'

'Good God Almighty, why on earth should she change her mind? A woman now, not a girl, marry a dull-witted, underdeveloped, penniless bloody actor! Of course she won't change her mind, she wouldn't be such a damned fool. Or perhaps you don't want her to. Cooled off, have you?'

'Certainly not, what a caddish thought!'

'Caddish be damned. In any case, aren't you being caddish? You promise to marry a girl, and in under two years you make it impossible for her to marry you.'

'It is not impossible.'

'That is enough. We will discuss the matter no further. Your mind is made up, her mind is made up and last, but I think by no means

Mother.

All my own hair.

least, mine is made up. I will tell you how. I want you to clearly understand this. Get it, if you can, firmly fixed in that thick head of yours. The day you walk out of the UK Optical Works to go on the stage and join a gang of bloody rogues and vagabonds you walk out of this house. Has that penetrated at all? Or should I say it again?'

'No, Father, I quite understand.'

'Right, I am now going to walk round to your grandfather's. I don't need your company and I have no doubt that you will be glad to be rid of mine.'

That is a fairly accurate account of the vociferous rebuff I received from Father.

Now I had Evelyn's mother to face and I did not look forward to it one bit. The interview with Mama was even worse than my scene with Father. Although couched in more restrained language she continued to make me feel a worm, a cad and a thorough outsider. I had, she maintained, ruined the best two years of her daughter's life. I was barred from the house unless I gave up this ridiculous idea and she considered Evelyn very foolish to have any further meetings with me.

In the next four months there were moments of happiness and much anguish. Evelyn hoped that our mutual physical attraction and, indeed, real affection would in the end break me down. And she could quite easily during this time have trapped me by becoming pregnant. But that was not her nature and I am sure it never entered her head.

One Sunday late in January 1924 the final break came. I don't intend to write about it here, it was very painful; there were tears and I don't think I came out of it very well. Indeed if I were to write the scene for the theatre Evelyn would stand stage centre as the good fairy and I would disappear in a puff of green smoke through the trapdoor. She was a dear girl and her mother was nearly right. I did in a way ruin two years of her life. But I heard that she was happily married a year or two later.

CHAPTER IV

The Theatre at Last

On Monday Mother was not surprised at my confession and praised Evelyn's sense and bravery.

'Now what do you propose to do?' Mother asked. 'Where do you expect to live? Have you thought of that? I will never be able to persuade your father to keep you at home. Of that I am sure.'

Well, I had an answer to that. My great chum, Alan Wilkie, from Highgate schooldays, was working in Ireland and for some reason his parents were very fond of me and very sympathetic when I visited them soon after Father's assurance that I should be thrown out of his house. They had said that, 'Should that happen you may have a home here; Alan's old room will be for you.'

Mother was most touched and grateful at this news. 'Now,' said she, 'this is what I propose. I am afraid that you are too late for the spring term. I expect the summer term at the RADA starts some time in May. I will pay your fees there. I will give you £3 a week pocket-money. But, from now until then, please save as much as you can. Of course, you will continue working at the factory until April.'

Eventually I arranged to go to the Royal Academy of Dramatic Art at the beginning of the summer term. I auditioned and was accepted as a student. Mother said I should now tell Father of my intentions to leave his firm and his house within two weeks. I must, if he wished, give him time to teach another employee my job at the factory.

The scene with my father was brief and to the point. He had been anticipating the situation and was well-prepared for it. There was no more swearing or any more abuse that I remember. He said: 'In that case you are aware, of course, of the terms of your resignation. You leave this house the day you leave the firm. That will be tomorrow. Heaven help you, I wish you no harm but you have chosen to make this bed for yourself and you must lie on it. I can only sincerely trust that it will not be as uncomfortable as I anticipate. That will do. Where do you propose to go?'

I told him of the Wilkies' offer. 'Really!' said he. 'You seem to be lucky in your friends. I hope they find your friendship worth while.'

I telephoned Mrs Wilkie in the morning and asked if I might move to their home that day. No difficulty at all and in I moved.

My first day at RADA was a wonderful thrill. At last I had stepped on to the shore of the land of my dreams! The remorse and misery of deserting Evelyn were beginning to fade and I have to confess that when I was introduced to my classmates, among whom were four staggeringly pretty girls, I began to realise that I might well find consolation. What a cad I was!

I spent four happy terms at the Academy. Except for two men, the other students during my sojourn there were younger than myself by several years. I was in my twenty-fourth year, whereas most of the girls and boys there were in their teens. I vaguely hoped that I might win the scholarship competition which one competed for in the first term. But I was not at all happy in the part I had to play for that competition and soon realised that it was not for me. However, I gave one or two other successful performances that term and Kenneth Barnes awarded me second prize as it were, half of Lord Cable's scholarship, thus reducing my dependence on Mother. In case my readers are too young, or have forgotten, Kenneth Barnes was Principal of the RADA for many years. Indeed he was in that position in 1914 when it was Tree's Academy. He was in the services through the war but returned to the Academy in 1919 when it became the Royal Academy. Incidentally, he was the brother of two famous actresses, Irene and Violet Vanbrugh. I never met Violet, but have appeared in two plays with Irene.

I was extremely lucky at the end of my first term at RADA to get a touring job. I started as assistant stage manager and understudy in a play, *Bachelor Husbands*. I toured with this for eight weeks which took me up to the end of the summer vacation.

As a result of these eight weeks touring, earning only £3 10s. 0d. a week, I managed to save £8-odd and I only backed one winner out of three bets. I was reduced to betting in five bobs each time! However, I returned to the RADA happily, not yet having to draw on Mother's three weekly pounds.

There were some amusing and clever teachers at the Academy. Rosena Philipi, a darling and funny woman and a splendid actress. If she were amused, her laughter would ring round the rehearsal room and it was so infectious that all the students would be rocking with laughter immediately. Another teacher was Claude Rains, whom all the girls were in love with. Claude was not a big London star while he was in England although recognised as a very fine actor. I saw him give a splendid performance as Casca in *Julius Caesar* and a really fantastic rendering of Faulkland in *The Rivals* at the Lyric, Hammersmith. I don't believe anyone realised the possibilities of Faulkland until Claude played it. I wonder, could the brilliance of Claude's performance have been inspired by the presence in the cast of three of his wives? His first, Marie Hemmingway, his second Isabel Jeans and Beatrix Thomson, his third. I don't know exactly how many wives he chalked up before he died, but I have an idea that he beat Rex Harrison! Of course Rex is not yet on the eighteenth tee so he may well hole out with the longer handicap!

Then there was Felix Aylmer who took the elocution lessons. An amusing episode resulted from an elocution demonstration given in the theatre on one occasion. Felix had set us various speeches from Shakespeare to recite at this performance. Parents and friends were invited and the theatre was pretty full. One fellow in the class, the only actor older than myself, was a small, dark chap and a wit. He walked on to the stage to say his piece, which happened to be Jacques' speech, 'All the world's a stage . . .' This was his interpretation:

> All the world's a stage
> And all the men and women merely players.
> They have their exits and their entrances
> And one man with his parts plays many times . . .

Here he made a brief pause, long enough for the point to get across, and it didn't take long. There was a scream of laughter from the students and, no doubt, many of the friends and relations. He managed to remain completely po-faced, indeed looked somewhat hurt. Then, continuing to the end of the speech, he made his bow to rapturous applause and laughter.

At the next elocution class Felix said to him: 'I don't know whether your strange rendering of Jacques' speech on Wednesday was premeditated or a slip of the tongue, but, with a name such as yours, I strongly suspect the former.' The chap's name was Handicock. Felix got his laugh as well. Handicock was a talented fellow; curiously enough I have never heard of him since those days.

Towards the end of my third term at the Academy Kenneth Barnes sent me along for a job of understudy in a production at the Adelphi Theatre of a revival of Pinero's *Iris*, with Gladys Cooper and Henry Ainley. Tony Bushnell was already understudying the juvenile, who had been sacked, and his part about to be taken by Ivor Novello. Tony remained first understudy to Ivor and I second. I also understudied the butler. I did not look very much like the butler, who was about six foot two, aged between sixty-five and seventy.

This was my first meeting with Gladys Cooper; years later we became great friends. Of course it was a tremendous thrill for me to be, even very small fry, in a West End theatre with this very distinguished cast. However I did experience one evening of acute embarrassment. At the quarter-hour Henry Ainley had not turned up. Telephone enquiries by the stage management established that he was indisposed and would not be appearing that evening. Gladys was warned that the butler, who was understudying Harry, would be playing the part, but in the flurry the stage manager failed to tell Gladys that I would be playing the butler!

I had ten minutes to transform myself from a young man of twenty-four to an old man of seventy. I plastered my fair hair with white greasepaint, painted dozens of lines all over my face and no doubt contrived to look like a very old white-headed chimpanzee. I donned my tail suit, and shaking like a jelly I arrived in the wings. The play had started, and Gladys was on the stage as hostess talking to a couple of guests. Just before I made my entrance I realised that two actresses standing by me in the wings were doubled up with laughter. This did not exactly calm me!

My cue came and I flung open the doors, Gladys had her back to me as I entered but turned as she heard my trembling voice (old age) announce: 'Miss Fane and Miss—'

I didn't get any further. With a look of amazement on her face she said, for all the world to hear, 'Good God!' The guests entered and I closed the doors. I have no idea how long the giggling on the stage continued but I was unhappy! I had several other characters to announce before my torture was over and on each of my further entrances no one on the stage dared to look at me.

In the middle of the last act when I had removed my make-up, the stage manager said that Miss Cooper would like to see me in her dressing-room after the curtain call. When I knocked on her door I was sure I was going to get the sack.

Gladys said, 'Let's see, Roland Culver, isn't it?'

'Yes, Miss Cooper.'

'Well, Roland, I am so sorry we all laughed at you this evening, but you did look very funny.'

'You see, Miss Cooper, I—'

'Of course I understand, Roland, but if by chance you have to play that part again, come on as the footman. None of that old man stuff. Quite unnecessary. Come on just as you are; you look much nicer.'

That clearly was the third actress I fell in love with. I thanked heaven though that Harry was not off again.

I believe I received £5 a week for this job, which was very acceptable and lasted well into my final summer term at the Academy. Once again I did not have to rely on Mother.

When I had nearly completed my last term, Arthur Watmore, who ran the Hull Repertory Company, saw me and Karlslake Harbord in one of the plays produced in the Academy Theatre and engaged us both for the season starting in September in Hull. It was a weekly rep. Of all the plays I appeared in during the next six weeks season in Hull I remember two, one entitled *Peter and Paul* in which I played Paul. The other I have good cause to remember as, at the age of twenty-five, I was a little young for the part. It was Ibsen's *John Gabriel Borkman*. I played Borkman! Again I had a slight make-up difficulty!

After Hull rep in January 1926, I started a tour in an American play that had been an artistic success in London. Of the original West End cast, only the leading lady, an old American actress, Lucille La Vern, and the original leading man, were in the touring company. The rest of the cast were recruited from English actors and actresses, with the exception of one old actor, who was an American, and the *ingénue*, both British residents. We all had a devil of a time under Miss La Vern's instruction, trying to become accurate with this very difficult American Middle-Western, hill country, accent. She was not a very tolerant lady. I played the family half-wit—a very intelligent piece of casting, no doubt.

This tour was for me a fascinating introduction to old-world theatrical environment. Apart from our leading lady, who was a real old ham, but very talented, there were two old actors, the like of which are now, I fear, extinct. They were real touring 'Laddie' actors. The first of these was, or claimed to be, an American born of a famous theatrical family. His name was Booth Conway. The second of these two actors, whose name I forget, was of the same pattern. They both wore pink-rimmed collars and pink-rimmed hairlines and only shaved every other day.

For those readers who may be puzzled by the notion of pink-rimmed collars and hairlines, perhaps I should explain that both are acquired quite simply by not washing the make-up from one's face after a play. If one does not wish to affect this display of pink, the normal procedure when removing one's make-up is first to apply a cream, rub off with a tissue or towel, then wash with a liberal application of soap and water. The pink collar brigade was averse to the soap and water process. Quite unnecessary, took much too long and closing time was fast approaching. They were not drunk every night; they couldn't afford that luxury.

I was receiving £4 a week for this tour; my two old actors were perhaps getting £7, I doubt that it was more. At the Saturday evening show these two old chaps were always drunk. They contrived to get into this condition between the shows. Consequently, their performances were not quite up to the La Vern standard. The Mid-Western Hillbilly accent from Conway became somewhat Bronx-side New York and the other chap rather east-side London. At the train call Sunday morning at the station they were always at their pinkest and unshaven. I used to wonder what the landladies at their digs thought about their pink pillows.

During this tour the country indulged in the General Strike. This did not close the theatres, but it made travelling for the touring companies somewhat dodgy. At the beginning of this industrial struggle we were in Birmingham and our next date was Southsea. On this occasion when we set off from Birmingham to Southsea, the management had procured a very small charabanc for the cast and understudies, etc.

The journey was uncomfortable, endless and embarrassing; embarrassing since the La Vern had a tummy upset which occasioned several delaying halts. At least two of these compulsory stops were on country roads, without a building in sight and the only privy for the poor lady was behind a hedge to which the *ingénue* would assist her. After a long and distressing journey La Vern arrived at her hotel.

One further incident, apropos of the La Vern's illness, occurred on the Monday night at Southsea. First, I am afraid I have to explain the final situation in the play itself. The juvenile leading man whose character was named Ruffe, who is La Vern's son in the play, leaves at the end of Act Two to fight in World War One, Soon after Act III opens we learn that he has been killed in France. The news is very

bitter for La Vern. For some reason which is now vague to me she
cheers up in the last few minutes of the play. Her last lines are spoken
stage centre, facing front; I am in the shadows down stage right
watching her and the *ingénue* is down stage left watching her. She
proclaims: 'It was sun down when you left me, Ruffe, but it's sun up
now.' At the beginning of this final speech the stage is sparsely lit, just
enough light to see La Vern, but not much else. As she says 'but it's
sun up now' a large arc light from the centre of the dress circle floods
her and, with her arms outstretched as if to embrace it, she finishes her
speech.

There had been occasions on some Monday nights of this tour when
the stage management had been pressed for time and some of the
lighting effects not thoroughly comprehended by the electricians, with
the result that the final flooding of our leading lady was not always
quite in time, and then there were angry words from La Vern when
the curtain fell.

Now I must return to the lady's indisposition. Lucille La Vern was
a Christian Scientist and on this particular Monday night she did not
feel fully recovered from her journey of the previous day. Nor, I
imagine, did she suppose that she had confident control of her bowel
movements. Thus she had engaged two local Christian Science practitioners to kneel in the wings either side of the stage and pray for her
during the performance. Their prayers were apparently effective, as
she did not, during the evening, have to make any hurried exits.

Came the final curtain and lighting effect, La Vern said, 'It was sun
down when you left me, Ruffe, but it's sun up now.' Up went the
arc light on cue to settle on the *ingénue* down left. Quickly realising
his error the chap in control of this arc hurriedly swung the light
across the stage on to me but corrected this immediately and finally
flooded our lady. It was the greatest disaster of the tour. The
curtain fell.

La Vern was about to have a seizure. But she fought this off and
relieved her theatrical frustration in a string of abuse against the stage
management. Said she, 'For Christ's sake, what kind of amateur
management set-up am I with in this production? No light ever hit me
until it was too late! What fucking son of a bitch arranges the lighting
in this God-damned theatre? What fornicating son of the Blessed
Virgin does admit to buggering up the beauty of the end of my
performance?' and so on, and so on. My dear father, with all his
Billingsgate vocabulary, could never have competed with this virago.
She continued to take the name of her Lord God in vain for some

minutes, whilst the hired Christian Science practitioners continued to kneel and pray no longer, I suspect, for her bowels, but for her soul.

I have no further stories of the tour of *Sun Up*. Albeit I think it proper to write an epilogue to my story of Lucille La Vern. She was a splendid actress of her time. Many actresses younger than herself behaved in a similar manner. She did her best to make the play what the author intended. If she considered that she was the main movement in the symphony she was, from her view, right. I have in my story made fun of her no doubt. Nevertheless, I respect her theatrical integrity and when relaxed she was a kind, if humourless, person. She must have died some years ago, but if she has found the world of 'sun up' I hope that she will be tolerant of my frivolous observations.

CHAPTER V

Encouragement and Disappointment

At the end of the tour of *Sun Up*, I was out of work for about a month. I had been conscious for some time of a niggling worry. My hair was becoming somewhat thin, and I considered that for a young actor to become bald would be a serious disadvantage. One could hardly play Romeo with a bald head and I rather fancied myself in romantic roles, so I answered an advertisement and sent my cheque to a fellow who absolutely guaranteed to grow hair. I persevered with the treatment religiously—an hour's boredom a day—for two months or more, then I decided that the chap was a swindling scoundrel and resigned myself to my thinning locks, hoping that with ordinary care and attention my hair would remain with me long enough for me to become established on the West End stage. It didn't.

I now had an offer of a tour with Irene Vanbrugh and Allan Aynesworth in a play entitled *All the King's Horses*. I was to play a young man or boy of nineteen. As yet my hair was thinning only on my temples and I could just get away with a fairly mature teenager.

All the King's Horses was a happy tour and we had a lot of fun, with many seaside dates, Eastbourne, Brighton, Bournemouth, etc. The weather was mostly fine on this tour and the four of us (there were two girls in the cast, one of perhaps thirty and the other nineteen and another juvenile man) and sometimes Toney (as we called him) Aynesworth, would all swim together. I suspected that Toney rather fancied the older girl, but I don't believe anything improper occurred beyond bottom slapping, which I observed from time to time. The girl would smile sweetly at Toney on these occasions and then, providing Toney couldn't see, turn and give the other girl and myself a broad grin and possibly a wink. It was all really nice, clean fun. Or was it? Toney must have been in his middle sixties at the time. He lived to over ninety and came occasionally to the Garrick Club during my early membership there. I got on very well with him on that tour. He was most kind and encouraging to me and assured me that I was bound to succeed. Cheering words from an eminent actor of his standing to a comparatively new recruit.

The tour finished at the end of September and I was out of work for a few weeks but, once again, not in the red. I then got the job of understudy to Laurence Anderson at the St Martin's Theatre, in a charming play by J. L. Balderston and J. C. Squire entitled *Berkeley Square*. The play was rather short and the management decided to put in a curtain raiser, a burlesque founded on a Steven Leacock skit of a Pinero play. I played the juvenile opposite Valerie Taylor who was also in *Berkeley Square*. Frank Birch who had directed *Berkeley Square* played the heavy. It was quite an amusing bit of nonsense although I don't think it brought the house down. But I was playing a part in a West End theatre and receiving £7 a week! On the way up the ladder!

During the run of this play I decided it was time to become independent of the Wilkies' hospitality. I took a furnished room in Percy Street, which runs from Regent's Park to Marylebone Road. The room was £1 a week and not too sordid. I had a gas ring on which I could fry up a breakfast and supper and there was a bathroom a few doors down the passage. It was not the luxury that I had hoped soon to achieve, but it gave me a feeling of independence.

When *Berkeley Square* closed I thought it was going to be the beginning of far better things. Basil Dean offered me a small but, I thought, effective part in a new play called *The Happy Husband* at the Criterion Theatre. I had a contract from him for £10 a week, double figures for the first time. I arrived a week later to start rehearsals. As I stepped on to the stage for the first rehearsal, the stage director called me over and said, 'You will not be wanted at rehearsals today and would you go to see Mr Dean in his office this evening at five o'clock?'

What on earth had happened? I spent a day of anguish and misery and turned up as instructed at Mr Dean's office at five o'clock.

Basil Dean said, 'I am sorry, Culver, but I have made a mistake. You are too small for the part. I admit that it was a foolish mistake of mine but in this play as the young gentleman burglar you are supposed to have overcome and escaped from Laurence Grossmith, David Hawthorn and Eric Cowley, all actors of over six feet tall, and David Hawthorn is a particularly massive man. With your physique I think it an improbable achievement. I hope you see what I mean.'

I then got my breath back and my temper. 'But, sir, I got your contract over a week ago. Surely you knew then the rest of your cast?'

'Indeed I did, but discussing rehearsal arrangements with Mr Blake I came to the conclusion that I had made a mistake. I shall be doing another production in the autumn and if you set aside this contract I shall naturally feel under an obligation to you.'

Said I, 'The autumn, sir. I have just turned down an offer to tour with another play in order to work with you. What am I going to live on until the autumn? I'm sorry, sir, I know little about contracts but I feel whether I appear in this play or not, that I am entitled to £10 a week until such time as I obtain another engagement or until your play closes. As for your feelings of obligation, sir, at the moment I need the money more.' That last sentence was unnecessarily rude, no doubt. But the disappointment was too much for me.

Basil said, 'Culver, you will be paid your contracted salary. I have met good actors and bad actors in my time, but never a ruder one. Good-day.'

That was that, but not quite the end of the story. About a month later when the play had already opened on the try-out in Southsea and was about to leave for a week in Blackpool before opening at the Criterion Theatre, London, on 16th June, Basil's manager telephoned me. It was the Friday before the Blackpool opening. He said that Mr Dean was not happy about the actor he had chosen in my place and would I travel up to Blackpool on Sunday morning, meet the cast at an hotel in Lytham St Anne's and rehearse there, have another rehearsal in the theatre on Monday afternoon and play on Monday night. If I would go to the office that morning, Friday, there would be a script there for me, so I would have plenty of time to learn the part.

The character which I played appeared mainly in a dialogue with A. E. Matthews, known to the profession as Matty. I told Matty years later during the run of a play in which I was playing a considerably larger part, that he was the most selfish actor with whom I had ever appeared, and on this occasion I received no help from the fellow at all. For a young actor on trial, as it were, with two hours' rehearsal, I was completely thrown by him and shaking with nerves. I gave a hopeless performance on that Monday night in Blackpool. After the play, the stage manager told me to be at the theatre the following morning at eleven o'clock—I hoped for another rehearsal. Not so. I was interviewed by Basil's manager who informed me that Mr Dean still thought I was wrong for the part, but, as I was being paid, he hoped that I would consent to understudy. Naturally I did not feel it politic to quarrel further with the great Basil Dean, and I said, 'Yes, I suppose I will have to accept that position.'

'Very well,' said the manager, 'You will understudy the part you were engaged for; also, Mr Eric Cowley, Mr Charles Laughton and Mr Laurence Grossmith.'

This grotesque assortment of characters I consented to understudy. At understudy rehearsals I had to dash about the stage as different characters, talking to myself. Fortunately, during the run of the play at the Criterion Theatre, something over a hundred performances, I did not have to appear for any of them!'

This was Charles Laughton's first success in London in a commercial play of this kind. He received wonderful notices. He had no scenes with Matty! I am aware that Charles Laughton had a wonderfully successful career and there is no doubt that he had an extraordinary personality, but he was not the kind of actor I admired. He certainly received an excellent press in *The Happy Husband*, but I thought he tore a passion to tatters. Also, he seldom looked at the actor he was talking to and played most of his scenes to the audience. I did not enjoy understudying him, as I was directed to try to copy his performance. It was fortunate that I never had to appear for him.

The Happy Husband closed on 17th September. I did not get an autumn engagement from Basil; indeed I don't remember meeting him again for many years. I believe the next meeting was during the last war when I was playing Lord Goring in Wilde's *An Ideal Husband*. One evening after the play a message came to me in my dressing-room saying that Mr Basil Dean would like to see me if it was convenient. I sent word that it certainly was quite convenient.

Basil came to my room and said, 'I felt I had to come round and see you, Culver, and tell you what an enchanting evening I have spent watching this very beautiful production. I should also like to say that your performance was in my opinion quite superb. Thank you.' That was burying the hatchet in no uncertain manner. If indeed Basil remembered that there was any hatchet to bury.

After *The Happy Husband* at the end of October I started rehearsing for *The Madison Girls* for three weeks. *The Madison Girls* was produced at an experimental theatre, The Playroom Six. I was the leading man and playing opposite me was an eighteen-year-old very pretty little actress in her first professional engagement, Jessica Tandy. It was not very long before she was earning considerably more than the £3 she received in that play. I have played in two plays with her since, *French*

Without Tears, in England, and *Five Finger Exercise* in New York—both big successes.

Soon after this production, for the first time since leaving the RADA, I had to turn to Mother for financial assistance. I had to have my appendix removed. She paid for my bed in a local nursing home and I was operated on by a Mr Barrington Ward. Not very painful and I think I was only laid low for ten days. Jessica visited me in the nursing home.

Soon after my appendix operation I started rehearsing a small part of a cockney steward on board an Atlantic liner in the play adaptation of the very famous novel of that time by Anita Loos, *Gentlemen Prefer Blondes*. I had gone up to £10 a week once more. The blonde, Lorelei, was played by Jean Bordelle and the brunette, Dorothy, by Edna Hibbard, both Americans. The brunette, Edna Hibbard, was the original Dorothy in the New York production and a very expert comedienne she was too. We ran only six weeks in London. Edna had a very good press. The play, however, was not well received by the critics; somehow the adaptation did not catch the humour of the novel.

The try-out for this production once again opened in Blackpool. On the opening night, the stage hands had not braced the set adequately. The scene was Lorelei's and Dorothy's state room on the Atlantic liner. The room was cluttered with Lorelei's toys and girlish knick-knacks, teddy bears, dolls, etc., which suited this coy 'dumb blonde's' baby-like character. Several of these toys were on the wall of the set on the side where I had to make my entrance as steward with a tray of drinks. Dorothy was on the stage by herself when I entered.

On my cue for entrance I couldn't open the door, it had jammed. I gave it a mighty shove and it opened but the whole of the poorly braced wall of the set shook violently and all Lorelei's teddy bears, toys, etc., were flung from their shelves all over the stage. We had been friendly and jolly as a company at rehearsals and I was happy and full of self-confidence, so that this stage managerial *faux pas* did not phase me in the least.

I put my drink tray on a table and whilst starting to pick up Lorelei's toys I said to Dorothy in my best cockney, 'I 'ope you're a good sailor, miss, I'm afraid it's going to be a bit choppy!'

The audience, realising what had happened, accepted the situation and I got a big laugh and an even bigger one from Edna. She then said, 'Well, I guess nothing's broken up, except me.' Another laugh, in which I joined, and that ended the *ad libbing* and we got back to the script.

Mine was quite a small part, but there were a few laughs to be got out of it, mostly fed by Edna, which, unlike Matty, she did professionally and generously. We became great chums. She was a most dear and funny woman, perhaps in her middle thirties.

One extraordinary incident occurred during the Blackpool week. Edna had given a party in her hotel on the second night, and I awoke next morning in my digs with a monumental hangover. I thought it a good idea to return to the hotel where there was a Turkish bath and have a jolly good sweat. In the foyer I met Ernest Thesiger, an actor many readers may remember. He was one of the English stars in the cast.

Said Ernest, 'What are you doing here, Roly?' I explained. Said Ernest, 'My dear, a very good notion.' I left him.

Some quarter of an hour later I was sitting naked on a marble slab in the steam room with sweat pouring down me, when a gaunt figure appeared through the steam with a small towel covering his loins, otherwise naked, except for a string of pearls around his neck! It was Ernest. He sat down beside me. He asked me if I was feeling better and I think I said, 'Not much'. Then for a few moments we sweated together in silence. Then Ernest laid his hand on my knee or just above it, and smiled at me, with no word spoken.

I looked at him in amazement and said, 'Good gracious, Ernest I thought it was palpably obvious that I am not that kind of chap.'

Said Ernest, not in the least put out, 'Oh, I didn't really think you were, but one never knows and there is no harm in trying.' We remained friends.

I could not resist remarking on the string of pearls and he explained that they were his wife's—oh yes, he had a very elegant and rather beautiful wife—but pearls, he said, should always be worn next to the skin to preserve their lustre. His wife didn't bother with this care, so he wore them and surrendered them on such occasions as she wished to wear them. Years later he acted with me in *Simon and Laura*, when I played Simon to Coral Browne's Laura. Coral asked me if I had ever seen Ernest's pearls and I explained the Turkish bath episode. She laughed her head off.

During *Gents and Blondes*, Noël Coward's big hit *This Year of Grace* was running at the London Pavilion and one day I lunched with Edna and Ernest at the Ivy Restaurant where Ernest introduced me to the Master. This was my first meeting with Noël. I was delighted but I fear I can't recall any of his *bon mots* of that day.

Ernest and Noël seem to have side-tracked me somewhat from my main story of *Gents and Blondes*, which opened in London at the Prince of Wales Theatre, where so many times I had watched Jack Buchanan singing 'Her mother came too' and my brunette doing high kicks in the front row of the chorus in *A to Z*. Now here was I, the other side of the curtain and the leading lady brunette taking me out to supper several nights a week to the Café Anglais, just across Leicester Square from our theatre. I may say her husband came too!

These were very hectic days for me, or nights, perhaps I should say. During these evening supper parties a couple of bottles of whisky were invariably consumed by perhaps half a dozen people on each occasion. I drank more than I needed or was used to, but I was very behind Edna's husband, who was always plastered by the end of the evening.

The cabaret turn at the Anglais at the time was an American crooner named Morton Downey, who sang to his own accompaniment on the piano in a high, falsetto voice; his favourite numbers were 'My Blue Heaven' and 'The Man I Love'. When he started to warble either of these numbers Edna was wont to say: 'Jesus, Roly Poly (I was a whole pudding on this occasion), this kid just breaks your heart, don't he?' and her hand would slip into mine under the table. By this time her husband was beginning to nod off.

Come the end of his turn at the piano, Downey, the heart-breaker, would always join us at our table and soon after we would all bundle into taxis and go to the large furnished house Edna had rented somewhere in Chelsea and the party would continue until the early hours. Husband would pass out soon after arriving home. Edna would then, with my assistance or more likely some brawnier male's, put him to bed. Revelry would then continue with Downey back at a piano. A bed would be found for me, some time near dawn when the party finally broke up. I would wake around eleven a.m. feeling not my best, and would make my escape about midday.

The two weeks' notice terminating the run of the play was pinned on the notice-board one Friday night. Next day I was washing off the remains of my make-up after the Saturday matinée when there was a knock at my dressing-room door. It was Edna's dresser.

'Miss Hibbard says please would you go down and see her?' said the dresser. I trotted down to Edna's dressing-room, Mary the dresser following.

Edna said, 'I'm not going out between the shows, Mary, so I won't need you until the half.'

Exit Mary. Edna then said to me, 'Shut the door, Roly Poly, better lock it.' I did so. Edna continued, 'Honey lamb, you're no pansy, but for Jesus' sake how long does it take you to take a hint?'

With that she let her dressing-gown fall and I was gazing at the full frontal. I can't remember what she said then, something about not waiting any longer, after which I was well and truly raped. Raped is absolutely the wrong word, I was a completely willing participant in this pleasurable exercise.

When it was all over she said, 'What a lot of time you've wasted, Roly Poly.' I protested that her husband was always around and that we had flirted at the Anglais but the parties at her house were always so crowded with guests that I had seen no opportunity of following up my natural instincts.

'Besides,' I said, 'what about your husband?' Then I do remember her saying, 'Oh, I guess I love the drunken bum, but, darn it, Roly Poly, I'm a normal warm-blooded woman.' Then she began to cry. I don't know what I said. I was deeply embarrassed. I think I tried in some hopeless, inadequate way to dry her tears. I was now desperately anxious to get out of the room. When the tears stopped she apologised for them, and then dismissed me something in this way, 'You're a sweet kid; after that romp you'd better go and put your feet up until the half and I promise no more tears next time.'

It so happened that there were only two more 'next times', as on the Monday her husband had 'flu and Edna would beetle off immediately after the show to Chelsea to attend to whatever nursing was required. I tentatively knocked on her dressing-room door after the midweek matinée, just in case.

'Come in, Roly Poly. Mary, ask Johnny [the call boy] to get me a taxi.' Mary left the room and Edna gave me a big kiss. 'Got to go and see the fella. You don't understand about love, do you?'

'I get a bit muddled at times,' I said.

She laughed. 'You're cute.' I didn't like being 'cute' but I had to settle for it. 'Now beat it. I'm not going to take off my make-up, just run home.'

Husband had recovered, I think, by the Thursday and was out and about, on Friday there was a party. So, off to Chelsea we all went and heaven knows what time we got to bed that night. Next day Edna and I went to the theatre together by taxi. No hanky-panky ever took place in the house. Now in the cab she made it perfectly clear that I was 'cute' again and I was promised no tears. So Saturday matinée was Saturday matinée.

There were several parties the last week of the run, one more mid-week 'matinée' with Edna in her dressing-room, and that was the end of my short affair with her. On Saturday, closing day, Edna gave a party for the whole cast in her dressing-room after the evening performance. Edna, the director and the stage manager made the plans for the party between the shows. So, no farewell matinée for me with Edna. I was alone with her for only a few minutes and I gave her a gold swizzle stick as I had noticed that she always, when drinking champagne, stirred some of the bubbles out with her finger. She, of course, gave me a present, a crocodile notecase, which unhappily I had stolen some years later.

Well, that ended *Gents and Blondes*. I had enjoyed it all. Darling Edna has been dead some thirty-three years; she could only have been in her early or middle fifties when she died, and she must have been an unhappy loss to the New York stage. She was a dear woman, madly sentimental, with a delightful sense of humour, but I think not a very happy creature. A splendid light comedy actress, with immaculate timing and it was a joy and a privilege to have acted with her. Finally, of course, she was generous to a fault.

After the run of *Gents and Blondes* I once again returned to the St Martin's Theatre. Paul Clift, who ran the St Martin's with Alex Ray, was always kind to me and fortunately also was a believer in my future success. This new production with Hugh Wakefield in the leading part was not a very good light comedy thriller. The play, entitled *Knight Errant*, ran only about six weeks. I had a fairly small part and understudied Wakefield. Once again I came up against a comedian who thought no other actor should get a laugh whilst he was on the stage, an attitude I have never been able to understand and which has always been against my own instincts in the theatre. But, unhappily, such actors existed. I fear they still do, but they would get short shrift from me if we happened to be in a play together today. I would rather appear with a performing seal than one actor I could name. No prize is offered to any actor who guesses the name!

Knight Errant was, I think, only put on as a stop-gap to keep the theatre warm for a play by Walter Hackett to be produced later in the year.

I was once again engaged for this play, named *77 Park Lane*, and it was produced in October. Hugh Wakefield was again the leading man and Marion Lorne, a funny personality, and an American comedienne, was the leading lady. She was Walter Hackett's wife. Once more I played two parts, and understudied Wakefield.

This production was an entirely new experience for me as well as for a great many other members of the cast. I do not believe such a situation could possibly happen nowadays. On arriving at the theatre for the first rehearsal we all discovered that less than half the play had been written! Hackett, it would seem, was trusted to write the remainder of the play as we rehearsed. The idea for the rest of this play (presumably accepted on trust by the management) was already in Hackett's head and, one supposed, would be completed on paper in good time for the opening of the production in a month's time.

Rehearsals started. I was again playing a cockney character. Two of us were discovered at the rise of the curtain serving at a coffee-cum-fish-and-chip-stall at Hyde Park Corner. After a few lines of dialogue Wakefield arrived riding on the top of a taxi with another actor, Wilfrid Blow. They both wore white tie and tails and both were drunk. Wakefield was singing and when the song ended the other chap gave the feed lines and Wakefield got the laughs. They climbed down from the roof of the cab and Wakefield persuaded the taxi driver to sell him the cab. The deal was fixed and they all came and had coffee at my stall. Marion Lorne then appeared, also in evening dress, and hailed the cab. Wakefield and Blow bowed her into the cab and Wakefield was instructed to drive to 77 Park Lane in a hurry. The cab drove shakily off and that was the end of Scene One.

In perhaps a week we started rehearsing the second scene of Act One, which Hackett had now finished. This took place in the entrance hall of 77 Park Lane. I was not in this scene, but as Wakefield's understudy I had to attend rehearsals. At a certain moment the curtain was supposed to fall and for a few days no more scripts turned up from the author. Rehearsals continued and the cast were becoming comparatively *au fait* with this scene.

Then Hackett turned up with another dozen or so pages of script and informed us that the curtain would not fall where originally planned, but the action would continue in the same set until the end of the act. A few alternations were made to the scene that had already been rehearsed, to fit in with the new situations contrived by this strange author. A few more pages arrived in a day or two with the words 'Curtain Falls' written at the bottom of the last page.

Surprise, surprise, there were also half a dozen pages comprising the opening of Act Two! During the final pages of Act Two various guests appeared, all the girls beautifully gowned and the men, including myself (now playing another character) all dressed in white tie and tails. These guests may have had a line or two *en route*, but we immediately went up a staircase to the gaming-room, which was to be the scene of the last act.

The management had contrived to collect a bevy of real beauties for the girls playing small parts in this scene. What is more, several of them had considerable talent as they were quite soon to prove in other productions in the near future. At that time they were all in their teens. There was Dorothy Dunkels, a very sexy brunette; Kay Hammond, a very sexy blonde, and Joan Marian, a brown-haired lovely. Joan was soon to make a name in films. Dorothy had several successes in the theatre and, of course, Kay Hammond became very successful indeed. Darling Katie we lost from the theatre through sudden illness some years ago. She has recovered her health to a large extent but I fear we will never see her on the stage again. John—Sir John Clements—her husband, has been a most devoted and patient husband through her long illness and I am sure that it is largely due to his care and affection that Katie has progressed as she has.

The last act of *77 Park Lane* was completed by Hackett about a week before we opened. The scene was a gaming-room, quite illegal in those days. Towards the end of the act it was raided by the police. But the proprietors had had sufficient warning and suddenly the roulette wheel and table were transformed into a sideboard, various gaming props were turned into something more innocent within a few seconds and the room became a small ballroom with all the guests dancing to a gramophone.

77 Park Lane was, in spite of Hackett's curious way of putting a play together, a big success. I remained in it for six months.

I did not know where to turn my eyes among all these beauties! Dorothy Dunkels, of whom I was very fond, again lovely with dark brown hair and skin like Desdemona's—according to Othello—I took round quite a lot. I particularly remember one wonderful day at the Epsom race meeting, the day before the Derby. I had been given two guest tickets for the Members Enclosure by my friend Laurence Irland. I even remember the dress Dorothy wore. It was dark blue silk with white polka dots about the size of a sixpence and jolly smashing she looked too! Although never betting in big stakes, I was still completely *au fait* with the form book. The previous evening I had done my homework.

We caught an early train to Epsom next day and I told Dorothy I had discovered a very 'good thing' for the third race, a horse named Chapeau. She was duly impressed. I remember that we lost a little on the first race and I suggested we should not have another bet until my race. Dorothy thought that rather a bore and had an each-way bet herself on what I considered a highly improbable animal in the second race and, damn it, it won her thirty bob! Come Chapeau's race I was amazed to see on the bookie's boards that it was priced at 20 to 1. I couldn't believe it. Were all my theories wrong? Did I really know nothing? I grabbed my form book and quickly looked it up again. No, no, I couldn't be wrong—breeding, weight, form, distance—everything right.

'Come on, darling,' I said to Dorothy. 'You are a quid in hand, shove it all on Chapeau.'

Darling girl, she didn't doubt me! I had £6 left and I put on £5. Chapeau won by ten lengths. I won £100, Dorothy £20. We spent a great deal of the rest of the afternoon in the bar, drinking champagne, and I hired a car to take us back to London.

To return to, or rather leave, *77 Park Lane*. I had been playing the cockney in the first act and a gent in the last act for about six months when Mary Clare asked me to play a leading part in a revival of *The Likes of 'Er*, a Cockney play which she proposed to put on at The Arts Theatre Club almost at once. Hermione Baddeley had agreed to play her original part and Cecil Parker was to play the other leading male part. Mary expected to get backing to transfer the play from the Arts to a West End theatre.

My bank balance at this time was in a fairly healthy state and I agreed to take the gamble. Paul Clift, who had always been very kind to me, agreed to release me from *77 Park Lane* and quite understood my wish to play a much bigger part, although he did warn me that in his opinion *The Likes of 'Er* would not be likely to get a theatre at the end of the Arts Club run. He was right—it didn't. All the cast, including myself, had a good press, but the critics thought that the play was dated. Yet the production was not written off as a complete failure and Mary still hoped for a commercial run. We, the cast, were prepared to go along with her hopes for a week or two after the play closed at the Arts. Then we all had other offers and were compelled to desert Mary.

Mary Clare was a very good actress but, I think, not quite as good as she believed herself to be. I sometimes became very bored with her criticisms of some leading ladies and her obvious jealousy. She thought she should be playing this part or that and not this actress or the other. It was a pity, for I believe in the end it made her very bitter and unhappy. She was splendid in *The Likes of 'Er* and was deeply hurt that no West End management would present this production.

CHAPTER VI

A Stranger Within

My next job was in a really terrible melodrama at the Garrick Theatre. The cast included Olga Lindo, Malcolm Keen, Reginald Bach and Laurence Olivier. I remember being surprised that the play received quite a good press and as far as I recall Larry and I were praised by the critics. However, my opinion of the play seemed more accurate than the press gents for the public didn't come.

Reginald Bach directed it and played an old man who had suffered a stroke and was wheeled about the stage in an invalid chair. Reggy was a man of perhaps forty and the character was about eighty, so that Reggy was covered in considerable make-up, grey hair, grey beard and lots of lines painted on his face. He said not a word during the play, the character had been struck dumb. Olga was the heroine, Larry the hero, Malcolm the villain and I, the half-witted brother whittling a stick throughout the play.

The melodramatic plot begins with Olga's character arriving in a backwood shack somewhere in the USA on a stormy night with a baby in her arms. She is taken in, in a charitable manner, by the family. I fear I cannot account for the presence of the baby, but it was perfectly proper for Larry to fall in love with Olga! Malcolm was Larry's and my elder brother, a religious Baptist who disapproved in no uncertain manner of Olga! When they are alone together in the Second Act, Malcolm, Olga, the baby and the dumb old man, sex rears its ugly head and Malcolm's religious fervour is overcome by his sexual fever and he attempts to rape Olga. The baby is dropped on its little napper and dies! Curtain—Act Two.

Act Three—complications are considerable. Malcolm accuses Olga of deliberately murdering the infant. Finally, Olga realises that the dumb old man is the only hope of clearing herself of this crime. Didn't he witness it all from his little cubby-hole seated in his wheel-chair at the side of the stage? Olga grabs the old man's chair and wheels it to stage centre with Reggy three-quarters facing the audience. Olga then gets down on her knees in front of the old man. Larry and I, by this time, are either side of the back of the old man's chair. Malcolm meanwhile, villain that he is, is standing down stage left with his back to the audience watching this drama. Olga then says something to this effect—on her knees—'Oh dear God, you know me as a truthful, honest woman, dear Jesus let him speak, give the old man voice, dear Christ.'

She then leaves God alone and addresses herself to the old man. 'Grandad, you saw it all, tell them, please tell them. Say you saw it all, tell them I am speaking the truth. Just say yes, Grandad, just say yes.' Then the miracle! The old man starts to spit and choke, choke and spit, gulp and gurgle and finally, after perhaps half a minute, a clear 'yes' and another 'yes' rings out!

It was a very hot June and it was very hot on that stage. Around the time that Olga started appealing to the Almighty for assistance Larry and I started to sweat rather profusely, as a result of desperately trying to control our laughter. We were seldom successful in achieving this control and by the time Reggy started to choke and spit, gulp and gurgle, we were both shaking with suppressed laughter and sweat from our brows and tears from our eyes would be dripping on to Reggy's grey head. Meanwhile Malcolm, wicked fellow, would watch us with a broad grin on his face, his back to the audience of course!

After a particularly bad evening of the giggles, Olga walked off the stage at the fall of the curtain in a towering rage and sent the callboy with a request for Larry and me to go to her dressing-room. We had anticipated this eventuality, indeed we had discussed how to avoid these uncontrollable giggles, but in vain. We arrived before Olga in her dressing-room and got the works. We were ruining her play. Our behaviour was unprofessional and unforgivable, unkind, also disgustingly rude, not only to her but to the audience who had paid to see the play. We really were very ashamed of ourselves. As far as I remember, from then on we more or less succeeded in pulling ourselves together but it was not easy.

During rehearsals for this melodramatic oddity, Larry and I turned up one morning to be told by the stage manager that for some reason rehearsals had to be cancelled for the day. So there we were at the theatre at 10.30 or eleven o'clock with a free day before us. It was, I remember, a blazing sunny June day.

Larry said to me, 'Come on, Roland, we'll get into my car.' (Larry had a car, I, as yet, could not afford one.) 'Let's drive down to the river somewhere and have a swim.' Seemed a good idea to me and off we went. First Hammersmith, then on and on up to the Great West Road, through Slough and Maidenhead.

About this point I said to Larry, 'There is a beautiful reach of the river at Cookham where I used to punt quite a lot. Why not stop there?'

'No, no,' said Larry. 'I know the best spot.'

So on and on we went. Eventually we arrived after turning off the Henley Road from Maidenhead Thicket at a backwater near Hurley. On that hot June day it seemed to me a very long drive for a couple of chaps to have a swim! It was a very secluded spot and we undressed. As I was about to dive into the river, feeling very hot and dusty, Larry stopped me.

'Roland,' he said, 'you see that tree stump at the edge of the river?'

'Yes,' I said, 'what about it?'

'That is where I first saw Jill in a bathing costume.'

'Do you mean to tell me that you have driven me about forty miles just to show me a bloody tree stump?' I said.

Larry laughed. 'Well, it's a very beautiful spot, don't you think?'

'We have passed others equally beautiful miles back,' said I. 'I am hot and hungry. I suggest that we now have a quick swim, then find the nearest pub, have a drink and some lunch.'

This we did. I had been rather unsympathetic. Jill Esmond was to be Larry's first wife and he was only twenty-two at this time. I should have remembered what a romantic ass I had been at that age, six years before.

Over lunch, beer, bread, butter and cheese, I had regained my sense of humour and we had a pleasant drive back to London. We had tea at his flat. During tea Larry put a record on the gramophone. What could it be but Hutch singing 'What Is This Thing Called Love?'

It was fun acting with Larry, perhaps too much fun, as my readers have learned. Although nearly seven years younger than me, Larry had been in the theatre several years longer and was now a recognised leading juvenile. I do promise my readers that I was not in the least jealous of Larry's position, though I admit to being jealous of his thick, wavy and lustrous black hair. My own fair locks were becoming very sparse by now.

It is sad for me that I have never acted again in the theatre with

him. I have always hoped that I might do so. I have played with him
in two films: one my readers will hear of later, the other I will mention
now. Larry was playing some kind of Russian diplomat. I fear I can't
remember the name of the film; it was made during the war, and my
scene with him was in a train. I was an English gent and I had a bottle
of Scottish wine with me and we both become pie-eyed before arriving
at our destination. It was quite a light-hearted comedy scene.
Someone from the Russian Embassy came down to vet the picture
before it was shown and they insisted that the scene be cut.
Apparently no Russian would dream of getting drunk with a friend
on a train.

Now perhaps I had better get back to *A Stranger Within*. Not very
surprisingly, the play ran only five or six weeks and then Olga got
some backing to take it on a short tour of seaside dates. I had no other
offers at the time so decided to tour. Larry, one the other hand, had an
offer to go to New York in *Murder On The Second Floor*. On the tour of *A
Stranger Within* Larry's part was taken over by Murray MacDonald.
Malcolm had either got another job or couldn't stomach the melodrama any longer so his part was taken over by Frank Pettingal, who
contrived to be more of a villain than Malcolm in the character, but so
wicked to the young actors as to stand grinning at them during the
final dénouement. Frank Pettingal was a dear chap but I missed
Malcolm; he was such fun. Years later in California we became great
friends.

The last seaside date of the play was at Margate where I met the
family Worthington. This Mrs Worthington had ignored Noël Coward's advice and had put her daughter on the stage. However, Angela,
the daughter, had come to no harm by it, indeed she was a promising
young actress, but she had decided on marriage fairly early on and
gave up her stage career.

I had been introduced to Angela at the Arts Theatre Club and after
the play at Margate where we were finishing the tour on the Saturday
night, Angela, who had been in front, came round to see me with her
sister, Elizabeth. We chatted for a while and probably laughed about
the play. Then Angela asked me whether I would care to join the
family at Birchington for lunch if I did not have to hurry back to
London the next day, and then perhaps stay the night. I duly arrived
at their house for lunch on Sunday and stayed a week! I am happy to
say the Worthingtons have been my friends from that day to this, so it
would seem that I did not overstay my welcome on that occasion.
Nutkin, Angela's younger sister, now Mrs Shaw, lives a couple of

miles along the Chiltern Ridge from our house, where she successfully writes novels under the nom de plume of Anne Morice. We meet frequently. I wish her well, but I do trust that she will never write a 'whodunit' play that monopolises a London theatre for more than twenty years!

During the short run of *A Stranger Within* Mother had persuaded Father that it was embarrassing, unkind and undignified that I should be compelled, if occasionally I was out of work and hard up, which was inevitable in my profession, to have to depend on the Wilkies' hospitality for a bedroom. Father relented at last and I was allowed my room at home when I needed it.

I had for some time past given up my room in Percy Street and moved to a more expensive and comfortable accommodation in Belsize Park, which was I think thirty-five shillings a week. After my week in Birchington with the Worthingtons, my prospects for the remainder of August and September were bleak. Nigel Playfair had promised me a goodish part in a play to be produced at the Lyric, Hammersmith, in October. Nigel Playfair leased the Lyric, Hammersmith, I believe in 1918 and in 1920 produced *The Beggar's Opera* which ran something over 1,400 performances and really set the theatre alight for a number of years. So at the time I am writing of it was fashionable for London actors to appear at Nigel's theatre from time to time, therefore, unless something very outstanding came my way in the next six or eight weeks I would have to turn down any offer that would interfere with these plans. Consequently, my Belsize rooms would be a bit of a drain on my resources, especially as breakfast at home would be supplied free—another saving!

On the day I arrived home I stayed in to dinner to receive the fatted calf! Father was very pleasant: he had by now become reconciled to the idea of an actor son and as far as I remember we never had another quarrel.

Rehearsals started for *Beau Austin*, the play I mentioned Nigel had promised me. The play was by Robert Louis Stevenson in collaboration with his brother. Bertram Wallis was the leading man and Marie Ney the leading lady. I played her rather unpleasant brother and Ballard Berkely played the unsuccessful suitor. Nigel Playfair directed, and played a gentleman's gentleman. Bertram Wallis was not a very good actor. He was best known for playing kings and dukes in musical comedies. A tall, handsome man and, in the picture postcard era, a pin-up.

It was an attractive production but, I think, a poor play. The dialogue was very stilted. Once again a situation in this play occasioned violent attacks of the giggles. Ballard Berkely and I had one scene together which we seldom succeeded in getting through without these attacks. What it was in the dialogue we found so unspeakably funny I cannot remember. I do remember that for a moment I was alone on the stage delivering an aside, Ballard makes an entrance, puts his hand on my shoulder and gives me advice of some kind. We stood face to face for a minute or more and then the giggles would start. We tried looking over each other's shoulders instead of into each other's eyes. That was no good; then I tried looking shamefully, in character, on to the ground. That made it worse! Actors don't enjoy this near hysteria whilst playing their parts but I believe very few have lived through their careers without suffering from it at some time.

About the end of the run of *Beau Austin*, Ballard Berkely, known as Bill, and I and two other actors, Francis L. Sullivan and Laurence Irland, with Bill's then wife, Dorothy, got the contract bridge 'bug'. Night after night the five of us would sit in Bill's flat in Brompton Road cutting in and out until the early hours playing this game whilst indulging in fierce bidding arguments, drinking, not too much, and smoking. I would frequently sleep in this smoke-ridden sitting-room on the divan bed once the game was over. As it turned out this life did not do my health very much good. Another bug Bill and I got in the early New Year of 1930 was golf. We even played on frost and snow-covered courses with red balls instead of white!

In the early spring of 1930 I started rehearsals for a war play, *Suspense*, which opened at the Duke of York in April. It was a well-written play about the trenches. The cast included the famous cockney actor George Harker and the brilliant Irish actor Sydney Morgan, playing private soldiers. It was of its kind a good play and the dialogue true and easy, but it was something of an anti-climax after the success of *Journey's End*. We did not run very long, about six or eight weeks. It had quite a good press. I played a cockney corporal and received a fantastically good notice from James Agate, which I well remember. He started with, 'There was one performance which seemed to me to transcend contrivance.' He then continued to praise my 'unique talent'. I very much needed this sort of notice to help convince Papa that my life in the theatre was to some purpose, although as yet not all that remunerative.

I was out of work again for a few weeks and golf during the day and

bridge at night was my life. I remember the only hole in one I have
ever achieved was at the fourteenth hole at Wimbledon Park, in that
early summer.

In June I started rehearsals for a try-out at the Arts, a play by
Rodney Ackland, *Dance With No Music*, playing opposite the very
beautiful Madeleine Carroll. We opened in July and it proved to be
one of those near misses. It received a fair press, but the story was
about a provincial repertory company and except for a cosy old
landlady, all the characters were actors and actresses. It is a fact that
very few plays about the theatre appeal to the public. Of course, there
are such famous exceptions as *Trelawny Of The Wells*, but we were not
an exception and we did not get a West End theatre. I, personally, had
an extremely good press and again a remarkable notice from James
Agate. The last sentence of which I propose another quote if only to
show later the perversity of some critics. After eulogising on the whole
of my performance he finished with: 'But this young actor is so
blazingly good that it is doubtful whether any commercial management will recognise the fact for some decades to come.'

Later that year I had my first film job; Sydney Jay, an agent of those
days, sent me down to Nettlefold Studios at Walton-on-Thames to see
about a part in *77 Park Lane*, the film verison of the play I had appeared
in in London, though not for the same part. In the film I played the
drunken pal of the leading man on the top of the taxi cab. I received £7
a day and over a period of about six weeks I worked some twenty days,
so I earned more per week than I ever had before.

Dennis Neilson-Terry was the leading man and Cecil Humphries
the heavy. We became good friends. They volunteered to put me up
for the Green Room Club and I was delighted to accept this invitation.
Dennis proposed me and Cecil seconded me and I was elected a
member early in 1931. After *77 Park Lane*, I worked in another film,
There Goes The Bride, with Owen Nares and Jessie Matthews, and very
charming to work with they both were.

Soon after this Dennis Neilson-Terry asked me to play in a new play
adapted from a novel entitled *The Rocklitz*, a period piece of the middle
seventeenth century. Dennis's darling wife Mary Glyn played opposite him. I had a goodish part but for the life of me I can't remember a
damn thing about the play except that somebody blotted somebody's
escutcheon. It was quite a lavish production and the costumes excellent; as I remember, Mary looked very lovely. Even so it was not a
success; we only ran for a few weeks. Dennis was a curious actor. He
could be very good in some parts and he could be very bad in others. I

am afraid *The Rocklitz* was one of the others. His father, Fred Terry, has been unkindly reported as saying; 'I have a daughter* who can act but won't and a son who can't act but will.' Nevertheless, Fred was very fond of his son but pulled his leg unmercifully in the Green Room Club. Should Dennis make a mistake at the bridge table, for instance he might say, 'Don't do a thing like that again, my boy, or I will tell your mother.' *The Rocklitz* was presented by Jack de Leon, the impresario who ran the experimental Q Theatre by Kew Bridge. I don't remember who directed the play.

In March 1931 I started rehearsing for *Black Coffee*, a Poirot play by, of course, Agatha Christie. *Black Coffee* had first been produced at the Everyman Theatre but I was not in this cast. However, it did not turn out to be a *Mousetrap*! Francis L. Sullivan played Poirot, I played Captain Hastings, Jane Milligan was the leading lady and Renée Gadd the *ingénue*. We ran about four months. During the run Renée Gadd was released from her contract for something better and her part was taken over by my friend, Angela Worthington. I was sorry to see Renée go but happy to welcome Angela. This production was at the St Martin's Theatre, my home from home in those years, and my friend, Paul Clift, the management.

After *Black Coffee* I played once more at the Lyric, Hammersmith. This time the part of Sharper in *The Old Bachelor*. It was a star-studded flop. These were some of the cast: Edith Evans, Diana Wynyard, Maida Van, Eric Portman, O. B. Clarence, Hay Petrie, James Dale and several other distinguished West End actors. We only ran a few weeks.

I am rather ashamed to say now that as a young man I found Edith Evans' voice madly irritating. I also thought her ugly, well, she wasn't very pretty! Nevertheless, by some magic in her make-up box she contrived to seem beautiful, but not to me when I first met her. I thought she was wonderful as Katharina in *The Shrew* at the Old Vic several years previously, so that when I met her at the Lyric I was very disappointed. I have seen her many times since and wondered why I felt so let down on that occasion.

Eric Portman I liked and knew well, but I can't remember much about his performance. I don't think that I was particularly good in my part; it was my first experience of Restoration Comedy and as yet I hadn't found my feet. It so happens that it has not been necessary to search for them since that time as this was my first and last effort in any of those comedies.

* Phyllis Neilson-Terry.

After *The Old Bachelor* I did several bad quickies. They were always bad, but they paid the rent when in digs. In May 1932 I again had a good part in a try-out at the Q Theatre. I received a very good press but the play did not work. We ran a week.

My remaining recollections of 1932 are rather clouded by the unpleasant memories of that year.

CHAPTER VII

Tuberculosis

The winter of 1932 was a most worrying time both for me and for my mother and father.

First, whilst playing golf on a damp day in November with Bill Berkely, I was suffering from what I thought to be the remains of a cold and cough which hadn't bothered me to any extent. I was about to drive off from the fourth tee at Wimbledon Park when I coughed a little and spat a considerable amount of blood. This frightened the life out of Bill and I admit to being somewhat concerned myself. We decided to discontinue our game and I made my way home, having another small haemorrhage on the way. I thought it best to go home and consult my parents about this emergency.

Mother was of course very concerned at my news. Was consumption a Culver scourge? Father had broken down with it in his thirties. True, after many months in Davos he had returned fit and well and had never had any recurrence, but my uncle Leonard had been stricken with the wretched disease and had died only the previous year.

I arrived home that day in the late afternoon and we decided to do nothing about doctors until the next day, after Father had been consulted in the evening. However, Mother did persuade me that whether or not my illness proved to be TB I should give up the furnished flat I had recently rented and have home care for the remainder of the winter. Fortunately my landlord was a friend and a charming chap and although I had a monthly lease I went to see him and explained my dilemma and he immediately said, 'Pack up your things, send me a week's rent if you can afford it and think no more about it.' I did this that afternoon, returning home by about 7.30.

Father was back from his work when I arrived and Mother had told him my news. He was sympathetic and practical. 'Got any money?' he asked. I replied that I had about £75 in the bank at the moment. 'Well, that's something,' he said, 'but if you have to go to Switzerland that won't keep you long enough.' Father had immediately taken it for granted that if it was TB Switzerland was the only solution. Hadn't he been cured there himself? 'You are unemployed just now I gather,' said Father. I said that I was, but had expected to start rehearsals for a new play at the end of the month, once more a production for my friend Paul Clift. 'Well,' said Father, 'it seems unlikely that you will be able to do that. However, we will wait and see what the doctors say.'

The following day our family doctor was consulted and he arranged all the necessary tests. It was established that I was in the first stage of tuberculosis. The two haemorrhages that I had had, the medical fellows said, were fortunate early warnings.

Switzerland, my parents decided, was the sensible answer and our doctor recommended the British sanatorium in Montana Vernala, called Montana Hall. This would cost, with the cheapest back room, £10 a week. £10 a week sounds incredible nowadays, then it was not. A similar establishment today with full medical attention, X-rays, the lot, would, I suppose, be something well over £250 a week. However, £10 a week it was and Mother and Father were prepared to bear the brunt of most of this; I would contribute as much as possible. It transpired that there would be no room at Montana Hall for three weeks, so I was to stay at home, and although not in bed all the time, I was required to rest for an hour before luncheon and two hours before dinner.

Mother and Father were faced with a second problem. For some months past my elder sister, Evelyn, had been behaving in what we thought to be just one more of her eccentric moods, exaggerated perhaps, but not, we thought, particularly out of character. All her life Evelyn had been desperately self-willed and intractable. She was a very pretty girl, not beautiful but with lovely big blue eyes and pretty mouth and regular features. Unhappily though, she had a bad figure, much too fat, with poor legs and thick ankles. For her stage career this was a great disadvantage. I think she was a pretty good actress, but her legs and figure debarred her from modern plays. She played in very few London productions; even if offered a small part in London she would turn it down to be leading lady in a No I touring company, if one was going. She replaced Fay Compton in several touring productions of West End plays. Phoebe in *Quality Street* was one role,

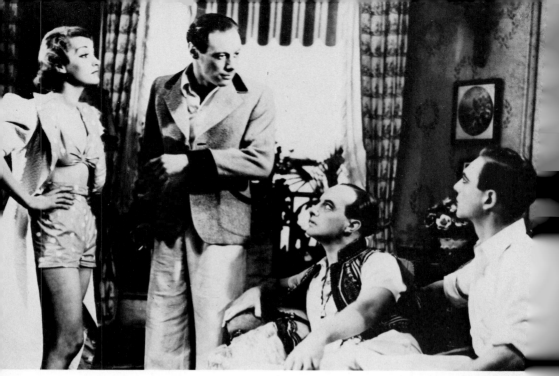

'Never, never leave me alone with that girl.' *French Without Tears*: with Rex Harriso
(standing), Katie Hammond, and Robert Flemyng (on the right).

'*Rather distinguished thing, Phipps. I am the only person of the smallest importance in London at prese
wears a button-hole. You see, Phipps, Fashion is what one wears oneself. What is unfashionable is wh
people wear. Just as vulgarity is simply the conduct of other people. And falsehoods the truths of other
Other people are quite dreadful. The only possible society is oneself. To love oneself is the beginning of a
romance, Phipps.*'
Lord Goring in *An Ideal Husband*. Townsend Whitling plays Phipps.

With Olivia de Havilland, Mary Anderson, Phillip Terry, Bill Goodwin, Virginia Welles and John Lund in *To Each His Own*.

en by some extraordinary
·lessness I fall off, or
·rly do so, but Olivia
·s me.' With Olivia de
·illand in *To Each His*
·n.

(*Right*) Breaking for lunch
with Ava Gardner during
Singapore.

The nearest I ever got to those lips. With Ava Gardner in *Singapore*.

'Look at silly little Roly in a hat, pretending to be a six-footer.' Left to right: Jennifer Gould (Willie Bruce's daughter). Bunny Bruce, Cash Hunter, Sally Cooper, Gladys Cooper, Willie Bruce, and Ian Hunter at Nan's and my wedding in California October 1947.

At the Bel Air Hotel 1947.

Mary in a play called *Secrets* another. These of course were costume pieces, long dresses, etc., and her bad legs were covered. She thought her performances far superior to Fay Compton's. Similar thoughts no doubt were shared by other touring leading ladies regarding original London castings.

One did not pay particular attention to Evelyn's changes of mood through the years. We thought she was, well, just Evelyn. She was different, and not quite understandable, a bit of a problem. For some time during this particular year her craze was spiritualism. This had annoyed Mother and bored us all. Evelyn was simply being more than usually tiresome. The wife of an American business friend of Father's had dined at our house with her husband and was mildly interested in spiritualism. Evelyn sensed this and seized on to what she supposed to be a kindred soul.

One day I was at rest before lunch, a week or so after it was established that I had TB. I heard the telephone ring and Mother talking to someone for rather a long time. Finally, Mother came into my room looking desperately worried, and told me that she had been talking to the American woman. She had told Mother that Evelyn was in her hotel suite and suggested that Mother should come and fetch her immediately, if possible bringing a doctor.

Except for the servants I was alone with Mother in the house. We were unable to get in touch with our doctor, but left messages asking him to call in a couple of hours if possible. We then called for a car and I accompanied Mother to the hotel where it was arranged that the husband would meet us in the foyer.

We arrived at the hotel and met the husband as arranged. He told us that Evelyn had maintained she was a medium and had gone into a trance or pretended to do so, and according to this fellow had talked gibberish. However he assured Mother that Evelyn was now reasonably quiet and that we would have no difficulty in taking her home. Evelyn was quite docile and came to the car with Mother and me and we started home. Mother was unable to accept the fact that she had a mentally deranged daughter and tried to reason with her. 'How could she,' Mother asked, 'impose on Father's business friends in this way, with this wicked, wicked spiritualism?' Said Evelyn, 'I've done nothing wrong, Mother, nothing wrong. I've been in a trance talking to Madam Alex. She died you know, dear Madam Alex.'

Madam Alex had been a nun at the convent in Brussels where Evelyn finished her education and Evelyn was besotted with her. Now here she cropped up again in her trance.

When we arrived home Mother said to Evelyn, 'I believe, darling, you must be very tired after your trance. Don't you think you should go to bed and rest?' To my surprise and no doubt Mother's, Evelyn immediately agreed. Mother helped her to bed.

Our doctor arrived in the late afternoon and after a chat to Evelyn with Mother he joined me in the drawing-room. He looked very grave and Mother was now in tears, which she did her best to restrain. Our doctor said that he would arrange at once for one or more consultants to visit us as soon as possible. I can't pretend to remember the remainder of that unhappy day. A psychiatrist arrived next morning with our doctor. After they had seen Evelyn there was a long consultation with Mother and Father. I was not with them at this interview. Iris arrived and we were together waiting in another room.

Apparently at this consultation with Mother and Father the psychiatrist discussed with them the pattern of the whole of Evelyn's life since she was a baby. His diagnosis was that she was suffering from a congenital sickness, brought to a crisis no doubt by her study of spiritualism, but he maintained that her study had merely accelerated the crisis and that her present condition was inevitable sooner or later. She was a schizophrenic and manic depressive and had never had a normal healthy mind. He advised that she should be admitted at once to the care of a mental hospital; he considered it quite unpractical that she should remain at home under Mother's care. Quite soon, he maintained, she would be completely unmanageable and possibly violent, and expert medical attention and nursing were, in his view, imperative.

My readers can no doubt imagine the heart-searchings and questioning. No insanity had ever been known before in either family. Would it perhaps have been Evelyn's birth? She was the younger of twins, the elder being still-born only a few minutes before Evelyn was delivered. It was a great ordeal for Mother. The birth of her first child. Why, why, why? this very religious woman asked herself.

During the following unhappy days Evelyn was certified insane and was taken to the mental hospital at Northampton. This was of course more expense for my parents, and an expense without any forseeable end, as the consultants could promise very little hope of a cure.

This new financial situation caused me considerable concern. I was supposed to travel to Montana Hall in a week or ten days and, naturally, I wished to take as much of the cost as possible off my parents' shoulders. I had been a member of the Green Room Club for just under two years. On top of one's yearly subscription members subscribed a certain sum to a Green Room Benevolent Fund. This fund was devised to help members who for one reason or another found themselves in financial difficulties. An actor could apply for a loan and his case was considered by the Committee and if found to be deserving a loan was never refused, and he could repay it only when convenient and of course no interest was expected.

I approached the Committee with a request for a loan of £50. This was granted immediately without question, in spite of my short membership and now, with the £50 from the Green Room Fund, I had about £125, sufficient to pay my basic expenses at Montana for three months, if need be. Even so, Mother insisted that she should pay for at least for the first two months and I should pay my fares and any extra expenses. So it was arranged.

I travelled to Switzerland sometime towards the end of November. On arrival at Montana I was vastly disappointed. Truly, one was about 5,000 feet up a mountain, but no sign of snow—indeed it was a nasty, muggy, drizzly day. Not, I thought, the sort of climate that was going to help my TB very much. I got a taxi to Montana Hall, perhaps a mile or so from the funicular. Here I was not disappointed. It was a splendid modern building with more the atmosphere of an hotel than a sanatorium, standing in its own grounds of several acres. I was greeted by Mrs Roach, the wife of the medical superintendent, and then shown to my room by the matron. I had just finished unpacking when a nurse appeared and asked me to undress, put on my pyjamas and dressing-gown and she would return in five minutes to take me to meet Dr Roach in his surgery. He wished to examine me before luncheon.

Dr Roach I found to be a charming and rather handsome man of perhaps forty-five. He had of course been sent the X-rays, etc., from London. He now wished to make his own check-up. After this, he told me to rest until one o'clock. He said I might lunch in the dining-room that day, but return to bed afterwards.

Returning to my room I looked dismally out at a dismal day. Then I rested on my bed as instructed by Dr Roach, picked up my book, an Arnold Bennett novel, and decided to forget about my depression and look forward to meeting other patients at luncheon.

I now propose to make what may seem to be an extraordinary digression. During my youth and continuing through my early manhood, in spite of being a poor cricketer myself, I was, none the less, a romantic cricket fan. Jack Hobbs and Rhodes opening for England, then Hobbs and Sutcliffe were my pin-ups, also Woolley, Patsy

Hendren, Strudwick, Tate, and so on and so on, were all my heroes. At the time I am concerned with, through the 1920s to 1931, I used to visit Lord's and the Oval continually to watch the county games and all the test matches I had time for. I was frequently accompanied by Mr Wilkie, who was a kindred spirit as a cricket addict. We would go to Lord's and the Oval together and though of course he was old enough to be my father, we were great friends and shared a love and appreciation for first class cricket. Sometimes in the mid-twenties, Mr Wilkie drew my attention to a young Indian batsman who he maintained would prove to be an even more notable cricketer than his famous uncle, Ranji. The young man was of course Duleepsinhji. His easy, effortless, classical stroke play was indeed a joy to watch.

During the season of 1930 or 1931 Duleep disappeared from the game. I do not remember that there was much publicity about his absence. Now I made my way down to the dining-room at Montana Hall and there, sitting two tables from me, was Duleep. He had been a patient there for nearly a year. He never played first class cricket again.

I met Duleep and the other patients with whom he was lunching, one a chap named Frank Randle. Immediately after leaving the dining-room we had a brief chat and I said how delighted I was to meet him but shocked to know that he was incarcerated in a sanatorium. He was philosophical about his misfortune. 'After all,' he said, 'I have had over a year to become reconciled.' I explained that I was under orders to go to bed and excused myself.

I remember being at quite my lowest ebb on reaching my room. There was this splendid athlete bowled out of cricket by this bloody disease, for I understood during our brief chat that the doctors held out no hope at all that he would ever be fit enough to play again.

Then my thoughts returned to myself and my own worries. Good God, over a year Duleep had been ill! Truly he was now out of bed and apparently only had to rest half an hour before lunch and for the evening hour. But a year, I couldn't afford to be ill for a year! Was this damn disease going to ruin my theatrical career, which was just beginning to show signs of life? I felt that I only needed one good part in a successful play and I would have made it. 'A year, oh Lord!' And what of my parents, with a mad daughter and a consumptive son on their hands?

Such were my black thoughts as I got into bed. Oddly enough, I remember that I went straight to sleep and was only awakened at about 4.30 when a maid brought me a tea tray.

After tea, I felt refreshed and in quite a different mood. One of the idiosyncrasies of people suffering from TB is that their spirits bob up and down like yo-yos. A year, rubbish! Duleep's must have been a much worse case than mine. Father had not been in Switzerland for a year and I didn't believe that I was as ill as he had been. No, I cheered myself up, I'll be out of here in four months, five at the maximum. Had there been a bookmaker around I would have made a bet and jumped at the odds of two to one!

The next day, after breakfast, shave and bath and back to bed. At about ten o'clock a porter arrived and I was wheeled in my bed to the lift and so transported to a flat roof where all back-room patients spent the day in the open air. The front rooms had balconies where patients could lie.

The weather had completely changed during the night. On the mountain not a cloud in the sky above us, yet in the Rhone Valley below perhaps at 3,000 feet there was a rippling river of cloud sparkling in the sunlight; a phenomenon I had never previously seen. Immediately opposite us across the valley, jutting into the blue sky, was the magnificent Matterhorn. In all a truly glorious view from our roof. In spite of my worries I was beginning to enjoy it.

My bed was wheeled into the shade. TB patients are not allowed to lie in the sun. There I was introduced to other back-room characters lying on either side of me—a man and a girl. The man's name I have forgotten, the girl's however was Pamela. She was a gay, witty creature and good company.

I think after about ten days I lost Pamela as she had improved sufficiently to be allowed up after breakfast until rest time at twelve o'clock. After rest she was allowed to dress and have luncheon in the dining-room. Back-room patients reaching this stage of the cure took their rest hours in their rooms. Their beds were no longer wheeled on to the roof.

I did not completely lose touch with her, as she would come up to the roof during the morning to sit and chat to me. Having now mixed with all the other patients whom previously she hadn't met, she had heard all the gossip of the sanatorium which she lapped up with great glee within a few days. Thinking back on the chatter of this girl and indeed her appearance, she very much calls to mind my dear friend Coral Browne. Pamela was a natural comedienne and provided me with many laughs and frequently charmed away my morning depression.

I was wheeled up to the roof daily for three weeks to a month. We were wheeled back to our rooms each day at about 3.30. The weather had been mostly sunny, sometimes we were in the clouds, but still very mild weather. One day on returning to my room I got out of bed to have a pee and looked out of my window; there seemed to be an excessive clanging of cowbells. The cows on the mountain slopes as a rule looked like very large toy brown creatures, quite stationary, cut out of cardboard, hardly ever a sound from their bells. This evening, instead of one or two of these animals, a herd collected by a herdsman was being driven down the mountain, presumably to sheds out of my sight. As I watched through my open window, I became conscious that the temperature had dropped considerably and I quickly hopped back into bed.

Soon after tea a nurse arrived and shut my window. She said, 'The wind is getting up, the snow will blow right in here; we don't really want a foot of white carpet in your room in the morning.'

When morning came I clearly understood the nurse's concern. Covering my window from the ledge was a mound of snow leaving just about six inches of clear glass at the top. I was delighted. I think I believed that snow was essential to the cure, or at least a great asset.

It now snowed continually for three or four days. But the snow clouds cleared and we had blue sky and bright sparkling frosty weather. At last I was allowed the up-patient's status. Up after breakfast and a quarter of a mile walk and back, then half a mile, then three-quarters and finally a mile. There was a restaurant and bar named the Mirabelle. At the end of the mile walk, the patient would halt and take an apéritif. Spirits were not encouraged. When I achieved the mile walk I used to drink Dubonnet and soda. I've tried it since, quite disgusting! But it gave me pleasure at the time.

My health continued to improve through January and by February I had attained equal up privileges with Pamela, Duleep and Frank. At about this time our librarian's health had improved sufficiently to enable him to go home. The librarian was a voluntary job taken on by an up patient. Dr Roach asked me if I would care to replace the chap. He said the job would entail perhaps an hour and a half's work a day, keeping the book lists up to date, noting books requested by the patients, and making a round of deliveries. For the up patients I would be required to have the library open for half an hour three mornings a week. In return for this work I might occupy a front room which happened to be vacant without any extra charge.

I readily agreed to this. The back rooms, although quite comfortable, had a comparatively small square window. The front rooms had large french windows leading on to a generous balcony from which one had the same glorious view over the Rhone Valley that one had from the roof. But it was this library job that before long brought me face to face with the one real tragedy that occurred during my stay at Montana.

In rooms either end of the floor to which I had been moved in the front, there was a boy of perhaps twenty-two and a girl of eighteen. They had, I believe, been married a little over eight months and had both broken down with TB early in the winter a few months after their marriage. They had both, unknowingly, been afflicted with the wretched disease before their marriage.

I am an old man now and perhaps it is possible that I am romanticising my memories of this young couple. I see them clearly in my mind as I write and I truly believe that they were the most beautiful young married couple that I have ever met. The boy, Hilary, had jet black hair, blue eyes, finely chiselled features and clear white skin, the faint blue of his shaven lip and chin somewhat adding to the attraction of his handsome face. The girl, Polly, had dark auburn hair, enormous green eyes with thick lashes curling upwards, a skin of white transparency that one sometimes sees on these beauties crowned with auburn and chestnut tresses. In the evenings before my rest hour when I delivered my books, Polly's white face would be coloured with the faintest blush which made her even more beautiful. Her nose was enchanting, slightly tip-tilted, her mouth irresistible, her chin round and proud. She was bewitchingly lovely and unaffected and desperately and hopelessly in love with her husband. Unhappily the blush which she had at this hour was the result of a slight fever that TB patients are prone to in the evenings.

Each morning at about 10.30, Hilary was wheeled in his bed down the length of the corridor to Polly's room and their beds arranged side by side, each facing the french windows. There they sat up in their beds happily chatting until Hilary was wheeled back to his room for rest hour at midday. In the afternoon he was again wheeled to Polly's room at 3.30, take tea with her and be returned to his room for the rest hour at six o'clock. This journey was repeated at 7.30 and they dined together. Then again he was returned to his room at about 8.45 and that was their day.

It is a characteristic of this disease that patients are particularly highly sexed during their illness. Even were this not so, one can imagine the frustration of this young couple each day, so much in love, sitting side by side in different beds, with the possibility of a nurse or doctor entering their room at any time, making it impossible for them to hop into bed together. Owing to the excessive expansion and contraction of the lungs during sexual pleasure the act is severely restrained in sanatoriums.

At the rear of the corridor dividing the front and back rooms was the ward room, occupied each night by the night sister, so that it was not possible for Hilary to leave his room and walk down the corridor to Polly's room. But love does not only laugh at locksmiths, it has quite a chuckle over balustrades, of perhaps over three or four feet which divided the balconies.

One bright moonlight night at perhaps eleven o'clock, a day or two after my promotion to a front room, I was lying awake when I suddenly became conscious of the faintest noise outside my room. Looking at the balcony I saw a figure cross my window, which I had no difficulty in recognising as Hilary. He was obviously climbing each railing on his way to visit Polly.

My God, I thought, how inevitable, but how dangerous—not the rail climbing of course, but the exertion. Then I became puzzled. How was it that I had never heard of these forbidden assignations? Other patients must surely have seen Hilary pass their window on his journey on previous occasions, yet not a word had I heard about it. It must be suicide, I thought, for this boy to leave his warm bed, climb across several balconies in the freezing cold, perhaps twenty degrees of frost, go to bed with his beautiful young wife, then back again to his own room. I couldn't go to sleep and was still wide awake perhaps an hour later when Hilary made his return journey. I did see that he had sense enough to wrap up well in woollies and a woolly dressing-gown, but no head covering—that shiny black hair glistening in the moonlight.

Why hadn't Dr Roach foreseen this eventuality and put the couple on different floors? Of course it would have been more trouble for the staff taking the boy up and down in the lift three times a day, but not, I thought, unreasonable in the circumstances. I puzzled and worried all this out until I slept, having decided to have a confidential chat with Pamela in the morning. She would not gossip, that I knew, in these circumstances.

Next morning after breakfast, I looked for Pamela in the lounge. She was there alone, fortunately, but clearly would not be for too long. So I asked her to come to the library where we could talk. I told her what I had seen in the night and asked her whether she thought I should tell Roach. Said Pamela, rudely I thought, 'You silly bloody fool, everyone on the floor knows, but it is a mutually accepted secret. No one discusses it. Tell Roach? Certainly not. Why shouldn't the poor darlings have their pleasure, they are going to die soon. Didn't you realise that?'

'Good God. No. Why should you say that?'

'Because,' answered Pamela, 'they are very very ill; both have had surgery. Polly has been given partial collapse of each lung and Hilary complete collapse of his left lung and his right lung is infiltrated as well.'

'But damn it,' I said, 'that doesn't necessarily follow that they will die if they behave themselves.'

'Roly, first mind your own business, there is nothing you or I or Roach can do for those children. Now shut up! You coming for a walk?'

'In half an hour,' I said. She left me. I got on with my job in a very gloomy manner.

Well, that day passed just as many other days passed in Montana Hall and once again I was in bed, put down my book, turned out my light. I did not go to sleep. I wondered if Hilary's visits to Polly were nightly. I was so hoping they were not. I stayed awake until after midnight. Hilary did not make his journey and I was much relieved. Indeed, in a week or two, I realised that the children rationed themselves and Hilary's journeys only occurred about once every four or five days.

So the days and weeks slipped by. I was progressing satisfactorily myself. Duleep, Frank and Pamela were also improving in health. But the lovers seemed to be losing weight. Polly's high cheek-bones seemed more prominent and her blushes pinker, I noticed any evening when I delivered her new book. It saddened me deeply to think it most probable that this beautiful creature might soon be dust and ashes. She was still gay and amusing about herself and Hilary, but it was never mentioned that I knew of his midnight visits, although she must have known that I knew of them.

I don't remember how many weeks it was before the start of the final tragedy, but I was directly concerned in it. One day, I was doing a morning round delivering and collecting books. When I reached Hilary's room he was in a black mood, quite unlike himself.

'What's up?' I asked him.

'Oh, Roland,' he answered, 'I've got a blasted awful cold, burning red hot pokers down my tubes. Crikey, I hope I haven't given it to Polly.'

This, I knew, was very serious. 'Have you told Sister or Roach?'

'Yes,' he answered, 'and I have been confined to barracks. Have you seen Polly yet this morning?'

'No.'

'Well,' said Hilary, 'I expect that Sister has told her, but I would like you to reassure her. I've only got an ordinary, bloody cold and I'll see her again in a day or two when I have got rid of the confounded thing. Just reassure her, Roland. I'm all right. Don't let her worry. You'll do that, won't you?'

'Of course,' I answered, 'at once.'

Polly never saw Hilary his old self again. He had no ordinary bloody cold. He had developed pneumonia. I went straight to Polly's room and delivered Hilary's message and told her not to worry, he had only a slight cold, but would not be allowed to visit her until Roach considered infection minimal. She had heard from Sister and was very distressed. I did my best to cheer her up, but not very successfully.

A few days passed. I was doing an evening round of collecting and delivering books. As I approached Hilary's room, I met Sister.

She said, 'Roland, don't stay too long with Hilary. He is very ill. I don't think he will want a book.'

I went into his room. He was propped up in bed looking quite dreadful. I asked him how he felt.

'Oh, bloody, Roland. Bloody, but I'll be all right. Reassure Polly. I'll see her soon.'

I made some facetious remark. I've no idea what it was, but he tried to laugh. Then he coughed a little, not much, but quite enough and suddenly started to spit blood and continued to do so when it became a really frightening haemorrhage. I rang his bell. I had no idea how to help him. The Sister fortunately arrived very quickly. She told me to go to the ward room and telephone down for Dr Roach, which I did. I returned to the room in a minute or two and told Sister that Roach was on his way and asked if there was anything else I could do.

'No,' she said, 'you had better get on with your round.'

Then came an agonising whisper from Hilary. 'Don't tell Polly. Don't tell Polly.'

'Of course not,' I said.

Roach of course had to tell Polly and she created such a scene that he was compelled to allow her bed to be wheeled to Hilary's room to be with him each day, only four, before he died in her arms. Polly died within three weeks, also having contracted pneumonia.

This tragedy cast a horrible gloom over the Hall for many days. Hilary's parents had been telephoned by Roach and they arrived in Montana a day or two before he died. His body was sent to England for burial and Polly's, later, to be buried in a grave next to her lover's.

CHAPTER VIII

A Bad Start to a Marriage

I remained in Montana until the middle of April, when Roach gave me a clean bill of health, but told me to look after myself. Duleep, Frank and Pamela stayed on for the spring and early summer, but were all pretty well when I left them. I kept in touch for a while. I lunched with Pamela some time in August and with Duleep later in the year. Frank I did not see for many a year. He was a Yorkshire man. About fifteen years ago I met him again in our local, the Angel Inn, at Henley. He had a nephew rowing in the Regatta.

On my return home I immediately got a leading part in, once again, not a very good play at the Q Theatre, hoping for a transfer which did not materialise. I was very hard up now and somewhat disappointed at the failure of this play. However, I was not out of work for long and kept the wolf from the door with several poor films.

In April the following year, I played in another short run, a revival of Pirandello's *The Mask and the Face*, at the old Royalty Theatre. The *Mask and the Face* was a translation of the Pirandello play by C. B. Fermald. Jeanne de Casalis was the leading lady and Franklyn Dyall the leading man. I played quite a good part but can't remember the name of the character. I thought the play very amusing and again disappointed that it did not run. I think perhaps it was in the wrong theatre. Both Jeanne and Frank were splendid. It was a light comedy with one or two near farcical situations. It is a curious fact that although, as an amateur, my first three plays were farces I have only appeared in one since. Now, having seen a couple of the latest in London. I hope to give farce a miss for the remainder of my career.

During the run of *The Mask and the Face* I played in a couple of films and made some needed pennies, but was still not really fit enough to act at night and film during the day. Before the end of the run I rehearsed for a Repertory Players' production. The Repertory Players was a society which produced a number of plays each year on Sunday evenings, usually by new authors hoping to sell their plays to a London management. The actors also hoped that the production would be accepted lock, stock and barrel and soon grace the stage of a West End Theatre.

This happy dream sometimes became reality. Indeed, in those days several Sunday night societies successfully sold plays which were subsequently produced in London. *Journey's End* was a very famous example which was produced by the Stage Society. The commercial production of *Journey's End* was not the original Sunday night cast, as Larry Oliver chose to appear in Basil Dean's production of *Beau Geste* which ran, I believe, only a couple of weeks instead of the couple of years or more that *Journey's End* achieved. At the time that may have caused Larry some regrets, particularly financial! However, it didn't make much difference to his career in life's long run, as we know.

Returning to the Repertory Players' production in which I appeared, during or just after the run of *The Mask and the Face*, I have to admit that I can't remember a damn thing about it, not even its title. None the less, it did have some effect on my life. I married the assistant stage manager, Daphne Rye.

Daphne was a pretty little brunette, or was she blonde at the time? She was apt to be extremely experimental with her hair colouring for many years, until finally she decided to let it become white, which suits her very well! Actually she was a natural brunette, with a lovely white skin, brown eyes which were very short-sighted. Maybe she had her glasses off when she took me on. She was a virgin of under eighteen when I met her and still under eighteen in early June when I seduced her. I am sure she will laugh her head off at that claim and maintain, probably accurately, that she seduced me. We were married in August. She was appearing in Terry Rattigan's first play entitled *First Episode*, playing the *ingénue*. The play was doing a short tour with Iris Hoey in the leading part.

The week that we were married *First Episode* was going to Brighton for two weeks. On the Monday morning I placed the gold ring on Daphne's finger in a church round the corner from her home in Warwick Gardens. After a small reception I drove Daphne in my new-old Morris Oxford down to Brighton, where I had rented a very pleasant furnished flat on the front. I was out of work at the time, so was able to stay with Daphne whilst she earned the money! Not very much.

Daphne, I fear, immediately became aware of my gambling propensities. There were, and doubtless still are, several poker clubs in Brighton, one of which I used to frequent. Whilst she was at the theatre each evening I would be sitting at a round green baize table. I am ashamed to say that on one or two occasions I stayed on late chasing money I had lost, sometimes retrieving it with interest. On these occasions Daphne might well have been home from the theatre and in bed for an hour or more before I put in an appearance. Not really the behaviour a young bride might be expected to receive with a gay laugh. Daphne didn't laugh and I don't blame her, but I somehow contrived to oil the troubled waters and we had quite a happy two weeks.

I returned to London whilst the tour still had two more weeks to run. I had taken an unfurnished flat, once again in Belsize Park, which I proceeded to furnish and get in order with Mother's help and had it ready for us to move into when Daphne rejoined me.

In the middle of September and through October I worked in two films, quite a number of days' work. Leaving home very early in the mornings and not arriving back much before 8.30 or nine o'clock and I began to feel ill and exhausted on these long days. Daphne, as it turned out, found that she had made a pretty poor deal for the time being when she married me, for, come November, I had once again broken down with TB. X-rays now showed a cavity in the apex of my left lung where the original weakness had been. Also my voice was becoming very croaky and it was established that my larynx was affected.

Naturally my family were in on all this bloody drama, and Switzerland was once more considered a must. Montana Hall was now too expensive, but our doctor recommended a Hungarian doctor, a Dr Mistol, whose patients were looked after in a very adequately equipped pension about two miles along the ridge from the Hall, so it was arranged that I should go there.

What of finance? I had very little in the bank. I had recently furnished a flat and acquired a wife. I was very, very depressed. Daphne decided to go back and live with her mother until she got a job. I borrowed the £50 again that I had returned to the Green Room fund, but once more I was about to become largely dependent upon my mother. My God, for how long this time? I was now thirty-four.

Daphne arranged the storage of our furniture. Somehow we came to an agreement with the landlord to release me from the remainder of the lease. Fortunately Daphne, not long after I left, got a job with Mr and Mrs Sterling who produced a repertory of plays, which they played all over Europe and South America in halls and hotel ballrooms and an occasional theatre. Poor Daphne had not enough money to supply herself with sufficient wardrobe for this job and I was obliged to find £25 to help her. That is all the money she ever received from me after the first three months of our marriage, except for my Morris Oxford, which she sold. Not another bob did this new bride receive from her husband for many a day.

It was considered necessary by the consultants in London and agreed by Dr Mistol, when I arrived once again in Switzerland, that my left lung should be collapsed. Of the several techniques used in achieving this, the simplest and most satisfactory, if there are no adhesions between the diseased lung and the plura, is an artificial pneumothorax. This entails piercing a hollow needle between two ribs and through the plura, than pumping air between the plura and the lung, thus collapsing the lung. In my case this technique was successful. The air pumped between the lung and the plura gradually disperses and, at first, one has to refill every two or three days. Later the lung ceases to put up such a determined fight against it collapses and the refills become less frequent.

As may be imagined my return journey from London to Switzerland was a pretty miserable one. In all my life I never remember feeling so utterly depressed. I had many times been miserable and often sad, but now this leaden depression I seemed unable to escape from. I was not afraid of dying; it never occurred to me that I might do so. I just felt desperately my failures, my financial insecurity, which had been more or less prophesied by Father. Now here I was, ill, married, unable to support a wife and within about £75 of complete dependence on my mother. I could see no light out of the darkness. On the journey I would pick up my book, read a page or two, and not take in a word.

Of course, a lot of this hopelessness was, I knew, symptomatic of the bloody disease, and I endeavoured to reassure myself with this knowledge: on that long journey to my mountain bed I was never able to snap out of it. What a blessing it is that this wretched sickness is now virtually defeated by antibiotics.

I arrived in Montana Village at the same time as on my previous visit. I found my pension to be a comfortable and well-equipped villa run by a happy French Swiss couple with their son and daughter. My bedroom was on the top floor with a balcony and a view over the Rhone Valley, similar to the front rooms at Montana Hall. On my arrival I was informed by the Monsieur that a taxi would collect me after luncheon to take me to Dr Mistol's surgery. Mistol turned out to be a very pleasant chap in whom I immediately had complete confidence. He proceeded to give me all the various tests that I was already acquainted with, after which I got on to his operating table and received my artificial pneumothorax. Mistol then gave me some unpleasant instructions. My larynx was badly affected, he said, and I must not talk at all until it had cleared. I must write on a slate all my requirements at the pension. He anticipated this enforced silence would last for at least three weeks, then I would be allowed to whisper. It depended on my progress, how soon I would be allowed to talk. Don't smoke, he said, if you want to live! I did not smoke another cigarette for six months. Mistol then escorted me back to the pension and helped me up to my room, undress, and get into bed, where I remained for over two months. Mistol of course visited me when necessary, bringing his equipment with him for my refills.

I was 'on silence' as Mistol had anticipated for just over three weeks, then on whispers for perhaps a month. By this time my larynx had cleared and when I finally spoke again I was rather happy to hear my own voice back to normal. I had been a very good patient and had resisted the temptation to listen to it before permission was granted by the boss!

Late in January I was allowed up with limited exercise. My temperature which had been going up at night and down in the mornings, had for a couple of weeks behaved in a normal manner and I no longer had night sweats. I still had three hours' rest each day. I played bridge in French, with some bed patients, two girls and one man who was an up patient. That was quite fun. The stakes were five centimes a hundred, so we couldn't come to much financial harm.

Daphne, having rehearsed in England, travelled to Belgium and France with the Sterling Company in December and by the middle of February arrived for a tour of Switzerland. Dr Mistol said that it would do me no harm, provided I had my usual rests, if I met her for three days. By this time I was having my refills every five days. Mistol insisted that I rationed our conjugal pleasure to one night. This was not at all difficult as Daphne was not keen to get infected by her consumptive husband.

I met Daphne at the station at Montreux. There waiting on the platform for me was a gorgeous redhead. I thought that she had gone a little bit far but red certainly suited her complexion. I stayed one night with her at Montreux, saw her play, and the following day we went up a mountain to Villa, their next date for two nights. We returned descending in the mountain railway together, and parted at the station, she to finish her tour of Europe, then on to South America for four months, I to return to Mistol's care. I didn't see Daphne again until the end of July.

There is little else of interest of the remainder of my stay on the mountain, except that I heard from home that Grandfather had died on 9th May. His death I have already recounted. By the end of April, Mistol was extremely pleased with my progress, but considered it best if I finished my cure in my native climate. He suggested that two months at Edward VII Sanatorium at Midhurst, to harden off, would see me fit enough to return to work. This was arranged. I left Montana, thank God, never to return, and proceeded home and on to Midhurst in May.

Edward VII Sanatorium was a splendid place, a large, excellently designed building. The french windows of large airy bedrooms opened on to a small balcony looking out on delightful countryside. I was still requiring my refills, by this time about every eight or nine days. Indeed, I had to continue with them until March 1937, when my lung was considered to be thoroughly hardened. When I left Midhurst these refills were given me at the Brompton Hospital, the time lapse between them gradually being increased to once a month before finally being discontinued altogether.

Dr Todd, a delightful Australian fellow, was medical superintendent at Midhurst. We got on splendidly. On my arrival he kept me in bed for a couple of days, as he said to give me a good rest after my long journey from the mountains, and to get acclimatised. After these two or three days I was again an up patient with three-quarters of an hour's walk a day.

By now the weather had become much milder and sunny and the early mornings very beautiful. Not only were there pheasants walking around but robins, goldfinches, greenfinches, sparrows of course, and chaffinches nesting; they would come to one's window asking for crumbs at meals, the times of which they had taped! The patients' nightcaps consisted of a glass of milk and two or three biscuits. The biscuits I never bothered to eat. The birds soon discovered this! No doubt other patients spurned their biscuits. In the mornings I would find an assortment of these little know-alls standing and chirping at my open french windows saying, 'If you don't want the biscuits, we do.' And they got them. Just after dawn they would begin their chirping until they woke me up. In May, when the chicks had hatched out and there were so many mouths to feed, they became bolder, coming right into my room even perching on the end of my bed. Indeed, one little hen chaffinch had the impertinence to stand on my pillow and give me little pecks on my cheek to awaken me! She pecked very gently, almost apologetically, as if to say, 'I am terribly sorry, but my chicks are hungry and really I do think that you have had enough sleep!'

I left Midhurst at the end of June or thereabouts. My life as a consumptive was over at last, but it had been a very serious set-back for my career; with the two breakdowns, fifteen months lost in all. I felt I was quite broke and dependent on Mother for an allowance until I got a job.

Before Daphne returned home from South America, I had had one engagement in a film and a contract for another for the end of August which would take me to the middle of September. Daphne returned and I met her at the station. I saw one or two of her company whom I recognised as they came through the barrier, then a pretty girl wearing dark glasses appeared crowned with dark brown wavy hair! The penny dropped, and I welcomed her home. Her hair was now *au naturel*.

Our marriage somehow survived our long separation and her extreme youth, but at first our relationship was perhaps a little strained, and who is blaming her?

After my film in September my finances had perked up sufficiently for us to take an unfurnished flat in a large new block in Abbey Road, St John's Wood. We installed our stored furniture and added a few pieces as the accommodation was larger than our first flat in Belsize Park. As you may suppose, after such an unhappy beginning to the state of holy matrimony for a young girl of eighteen—three months home with her husband then nine months' separation with a brief meeting in Switzerland half way through my cure—was, to say the least, frustrating and unsettling.

Immediately after my film finished in mid-September, I rehearsed a new play by a new author, James Parish, *Distinguished Gathering*. This was a thriller and was produced experimentally at the Embassy Theatre at Swiss Cottage. For once this experimental engagement was an immediate success and was bought and presented, once again for me, at the St Martin's Theatre. We opened in November with the original cast except for poor Bernard Lee playing the leading man, who had received excellent notices at the Embassy. The management did not consider that he had a big enough name at the time and Frank

Vosper played his part in London. A cruel disappointment for Bernie, but the sort of frustrating episode to which many actors have to reconcile themselves during their early struggles up the ladder of this, sometimes, most unkind profession.

I played the villain in this piece and once again received a good press and James Agate joined the acclaim. The play ran, I think, five months; I know it took me to about the beginning of April.

In April I once again returned to work on the silver screen. The new film that I was engaged for I do remember the title, the producer, director, and most of the cast. The title was *Accused*. My good friend Harold French was dialogue director and was also trusted with most of the casting. He recommended me for, once again, a villain. Although I remember the cast, I remember little of the plot of the film; its location was France, there was a murder in the story for which an innocent defendant was accused and tried in a French court. Whether the innocent prisoner in the dock was Douglas Fairbanks Junior, the hero, or Dolores del Rio, the heroine, I fear I cannot say, neither can I tell whether Leo Genn was the Counsel for the defence or prosecution, or whether it was Basil Sidney—they were one or the other. I played a nasty chap and I remember threatening my wife, Florence Desmond, with a revolver, but whether I shot her or not I've no idea. It is possible that I did and that was what all the fuss was about and the wrong person accused of the crime.

I acquired a lot of new friends whilst making this picture. First Doug Fairbanks. If you become his friend then you have a friend for life. Whenever he has happened to be in front at any play I have been in, he always appears in my dressing-room at the end of the show, flashing those fine teeth in a broad grin exactly like his father's and we have a chat and drink together. But I have never been in a film or play with him since. A pity.

Then there was T. Freeland, the director with whom I worked in another picture later, a dear chap. Marcel Hellman was the producer—he again employed me in several other pictures. Flo Desmond, whom I frequently see on visits to the South of France where she has a villa. Harold French was, of course, a friend of mine at the Green Room Club. Basil Sidney and Leo Genn I already knew also. However, one member of the cast whom I had never met before was Googie Withers, playing a small part. She was very young at the time, perhaps seventeen. Since then I have had the pleasure of playing with her in two plays, and one film, *On Approval*, which I will come to later.

Accused kept me at work until some time in May. I then had several weeks of unemployment. However, I was still having a few bets on the gees and holding my own, also more than holding my own at the poker table at the Green Room, another fortunate run of cards. Nevertheless, no sign of more work until the middle of July when I did a couple of quickies for Warner Brothers. (Quickies as a rule were made in five days and I think I was paid £50). Daphne decided that she had better earn some money herself, as this somewhat unreliable husband was barely keeping the wolf from the door, so towards the end of August we were separated again, and she took a job in a repertory company operating at Margate. I visited her there in her digs whenever I had some spare cash. She remained in this rep until the end of November, when I told her to give in her notice as I was now in the money at last.

CHAPTER IX

French Without Tears

One afternoon in the middle of October 1936, I was playing bridge in the Green Room when Harold French called me aside as I was cut out of the table, and told me to go and see Bronson Albery at his office in Wyndham's Theatre at four o'clock. There was, he said, a possible job for me in a play that he was going to direct. I duly turned up to see Bronny, as I later called him, on the dot of four o'clock. Bronny said that he and some others were about to produce a new play by a comparatively unknown author, one Terence Rattigan, and that Harold French had suggested that I would be right for the part of a Naval Commander.

'Just read the script this afternoon and see if you think you can make a go of the character. It is a good part,' he said. 'I shall be in this office until after six, you can easily read it by then. Come back and tell me what you think.'

I read it at once. It was not only a good part but, I thought, a very good play and extremely funny. I hustled back to Wyndham's Theatre and told Bronny that I thought it an extremely funny play and I was certain that I could more than make a go of Commander Rogers. I was engaged, salary £20 a week. That, of course, sounds chicken-feed nowadays, but not then. It was by no means a large salary, but I don't believe anyone in that cast received as much as £50.

I was thrilled. I was certain that the play could not fail. This time I was right. It was *French Without Tears*. When I read it, it had some quite different name, and although that rose would have smelt as sweet under its original title, *French Without Tears* probably gave it a more provocative scent.

I returned from Bronny to the Green Room where I saw Harold and thanked him. He asked me what I thought of the play and I told him that I believed it the best light comedy that I had ever read. He told me some of the cast, Kay Hammond, Rex Harrison, Robert Flemyng, Jessica Tandy and Trevor Howard (Guy Middleton had not yet been cast), all of whom I knew except Trevor, who was only twenty.

I then said, 'Dear boy, we are on a certainty.'

'Don't get over-excited,' he said, 'you should know that nothing is certain in our job, but I think we have an excellent chance.'

Rehearsals were fun, but there was one heartbreak. Alec Archdale, whom Bronny had cast for the part of Brian, was quite wrong for the role and Harold had to sack him and Guy Middleton, who was perfect casting, played the part. Alec Archdale is dead now so I don't suppose he cares any more. So incidentally is Guy! Oh dear! So many of my characters are dead it is absolutely beastly and I am hardly half way through my history! I wonder if Ladbroke's are going to win after all? Never mind, let's get back to *French Without Tears* rehearsals.

We all enjoyed these days and had a lot of laughs. There was one particularly amusing incident which occurred at about the third rehearsal, when we rehearsed the second act for the first time. For some reason Rex was not with us. In the role of the Commander I make an entrance with Katie while Rex's character is sitting more or less facing the audience. As we enter I am telling Katie a story: my line is, 'And I gave the order all hands on deck' and Rex's line is, 'And did they come?'

In Rex's absence Katie said to Harold in that curious, delicious and provocative voice, 'Harold darling. Don't you think it would be better if I said that line?'

Harold said, 'All right, Katie, go ahead.'

When we next rehearsed that act with Rex we arrived at this situation and before Rex had a chance to say the line Katie said it.

'Here, just a minute,' said Rex, 'that's my line.'

'Well, darling,' said Katie, 'Harold thought it better if I said it.'

Harold said, 'Come, come, Katie, *you* thought it better.'

'Did I?' said Katie. 'Well, you thought so too, didn't you?'

'To be honest,' said Harold, 'I said you might say it because I looked forward to seeing what would happen when Rex turned up at the next rehearsal.'

Rex said the line.

During these rehearsals we were all pretty sure of ourselves and thought the play charming and very funny, so at the dress rehearsal we were all pretty confident, but it was ghastly. There were about a dozen or so people in front watching and none of them laughed at all.

It was very depressing. Indeed so depressing for nearly everyone that one of the backers sold out his shares to a more optimistic chap. The pessimist must have kicked himself very hard the next evening.

In his memoirs, *I Thought I Never Could*, Harold French tells how he made us all do it over again and pull our socks up. But we went home that night not quite so cock-a-hoop as we had been during rehearsals.

Most readers interested in the theatre know of the enormous success of *French Without Tears*, but perhaps they don't know the supreme thrill all the cast, the young author, and director Harold felt as the curtain fell to thunderous applause and laughter on that first night. Down came the curtain, up it went again, down, up, down, up, heaven knows how many times. Bronny Albery came round to see us all and I remember he said, 'Well, it looks as though you will be here for some time.' I was in it for two and a half years.

On opening night Mother and Father and Iris were in the stalls and were delighted. Daphne could not join in the thrill of that evening as she was playing at Margate. After my family left my dressing-room there were still dozens of characters around back stage, full of congratulations and I gradually got full of whisky. Finally, with several others, I went to the Savoy Grill for supper. I remember waking on the following morning with a monumental hangover; I didn't mind, and it didn't last long—I was too happy.

The critics were unanimous in their praise, both of the play and the acting. Later the evening papers joined in the acclaim. *French Without Tears* immediately started playing to packed houses. Then came the Sunday papers, again unanimity. Except for, guess who, James Agate! Here, this fellow who had been singing my praises in every play I had appeared in for some years, now that I had, as it were, hit the jackpot in a success, the like of which I would be very lucky to repeat for many a day, he pans it! Actually, I don't think he bothered even to mention me or any of the cast. He just maintained that the play was piffling rubbish. I don't remember his actual words, but he was quite vitriolic about it. What is more, he would not stop worrying this bone of contention. For several Sundays he would return to the subject. He thought it a sad reflection on the British stage that the public had nothing better to do than pack out the Criterion Theatre. However, the public took little notice of Agate's tirades, if indeed they bothered to read them. They still swarmed to the box office in Piccadilly Circus. At last I felt I was established in the West End theatre. I think I should say here, that through my career, I have not found all critics as perverse as I considered James Agate on this occasion, indeed many have been consistent in praising my work. Particularly I should like to take this opportunity of thanking Sir Harold Hobson for his unremitting acclaim of my efforts through the years, be the play he might be reviewing poor or good.

All our contracts in *French Without Tears* were for the run of the play except for Jessica Tandy who somehow managed to procure a contract with a release clause of four months, which she took advantage of when the time came. Leneen MacGrath replaced her and gave a charming performance. Only Guy Middleton, Trevor Howard, Percy Walsh and myself completed the two and a half years' run.

In the first act of the play Katie wore a two-piece bathing suit (not a bikini—they had not as yet appeared to disclose most of the female form divine), but a costume as brief as was acceptable in those days; a fair portion of her pretty figure was exposed between her hips and her top covering. One evening around January 1938, in her dressing-room I said: 'Putting on a tiny bit of weight, aren't you darling?' 'Oh, you beast,' said Katie. 'You would be the first to notice. Does it show much?' Said I, 'Well, love, you do seem to be losing some of that delightfully svelte figure that I have always admired. When will you be leaving us?' She departed at the end of the month. Her second son was born at the end of May.

Rex also left sometime in 1938. He had wanted to leave for some time. Rex is a character who has, through life, usually managed to get his own way. I don't know why the management released him; he clearly was not in the family way! Later, towards the end of the year, Bobby Flemyng also contrived to make his exit, I have no idea how. I was offered a very good part in a film in November 1938, but they would not accept me whilst in the play because the film called for three weeks' work on location somewhere in Cornwall. My request to leave the cast was turned down flat. Maybe it was just as well, as finally at the end of the run, Guy and I were the only members of the cast chosen to play in the film, which was as successful as the play, and as useful to my career as the play had been.

After Katie left us the atmosphere backstage was never quite the same. Some *joie de vivre* had evaporated with her exit. We did have enormous fun during the first year of *French Without Tears*, sometimes too much between ourselves, I regret to admit, without letting the audience in on our jokes.

In one scene that I played with Katie, she would endeavour to dry me up (make me laugh). She never succeeded, but she persevered. We sat on a bench parallel to the footlights facing the audience. The dialogue went this way. I said, 'Diana, is your feeling for me just infatuation or do you really, really love me?' Katie (Diana) replied, 'But of course I love you, Bill.' At this moment during her line Katie would appear to see a bit of fluff or thread of cotton somewhere on my clothes, perhaps my trousers, in an embarrassing place or maybe on my coat at the furthest point from her. This imaginary piece of rubbish she would reach across and pick off with finger and thumb and delicately deposit on the floor.

One day I decided that she should have something visible to remove. I confided my intention to the rest of the cast who gathered in the wings to watch the result. I had sewn a piece of pale blue cotton through the lapel of my blue blazer on the furthest side from Katie, the remainder of the cotton, perhaps a yard or more, went into the inside pocket of the jacket. While Katie and I waited in the 'garden' together for our entrance, I took care that she did not see the cotton until we entered through the french windows. I have a line to Katie, then Rex who is alone on the stage has a line, I another, Rex another and he exits. During this exchange I allowed Katie to see the short thread of cotton.

She took the bait, hook, line and sinker. I saw her great blue orbs light up. We then sat on the bench and arrived at Katie's line, 'Of course I love you, Bill.' Her pretty little arm reached across my manly chest and her finger and thumb picked off the cotton. She pulled perhaps a foot or more, then said, 'Oh, my God,' and tried to push it back. She thought she was unravelling the lining of my coat. I regret to say very little of the remainder of the scene was spoken. Rex and Guy entered, Katie made her exit and we could all hear her laughter across the back of the stage right to her dressing-room.

I didn't get away with that one. The stage director, quite rightly, reported the incident to the manager and I was required to present myself to Bronny Albery in his office at Wyndham's Theatre, where I received a thorough dressing down. Even so, at the end of the first year's run, I was given a rise of £5 a week!

I should report one other occasion of uncontrolled laughter for which I fear I was again responsible. But on this occasion I was completely innocent of intent to provoke this near hysteria. Indeed, the audience were in on the joke and laughed even more than the two actors involved. Once again this happened in the second act.

I was wearing white linen trousers, a short sports shirt and a double-breasted blue blazer. All the characters in the play were going to a fancy dress gala and were dressed up in various costumes. Bobby

Flemyng, with whom I was about to have a quarrel scene over Katie, was wearing a Greek Evzones uniform, the Greek Highland Regiment. At the start of the quarrel, apparently about to develop into fisticuffs, Bobby was standing behind a sofa with a high back which concealed the lower half of this tall chap from my view. At the heated climax of this quarrel I say, 'All right, put your fists up.' I then rip off my double-breasted jacket, throw it aside and face Bobby who leaps over the sofa displaying this curious short white voluminous skirt and his long bare legs. This strange sight my character finds highly amusing, and he forgets our quarrel and bursts into laughter.

On this occasion I ripped off my coat, Bobby leapt over the sofa and faced me and a look of horror and then amazement appeared on his face, followed by a broad grin. It took me but a tenth of a second to look down in the direction of his gaze, and I discovered that the top button only of my fly was fastened, not another button was done up! I flopped into an armchair in extreme embarrassment, crossed my legs, and endeavoured unobtrusively to button my fly. Bobby collapsed on the sofa and the audience almost immediately caught on and the laughter at my expense was uncontrollable.

I did my best to pretend that nothing untoward had occurred and tried to continue with the scene whilst performing the most extraordinary contortions hoping to conceal my dressing which should have been completed in my room. It was no good, the more I tried to carry on the less Bobby was able to control himself, and the more the audience laughed. Eventually, I somehow succeeded in doing up the last button and rose to my feet amidst loud laughter and applause, Bobby still speechless and the scene never completed. Should any of my readers have the misfortune to enter a room full of people and discover your fly to be unbuttoned, I will lay you a long shade of odds that if you sit down in an armchair and endeavour to correct this social blot without being observed, you will not achieve the required result.

Sometime in September 1937 Daphne decided to become pregnant and Michael, my elder son, was born the following June, a few days or weeks after Katie's Timothy. They indulged in a kind of race which Katie won! I didn't have a bet on it.

At the end of January 1938 Daphne and I decided that our present accommodation in Abbey Road was clearly inadequate for a baby and nanny which would shortly be part of our household. We found a very comfortable, well-equipped maisonette in a converted house in East Heath Road, facing Hampstead Heath. Of course there was more furniture to buy, curtains, carpets, etc. However, owing to my phenomenal run of luck at cards over the last months I had a pretty solid bank balance, and the new furnishings were no problem. We moved into our new home in March and Michael was born on 16th June, and took a devil of a time arriving. I sat up all night. The doctor who delivered our infant had, I think over-doped Daphne and she gave up trying. The boy eventually arrived by which time, perhaps as a result of too many large ones, I think I felt worse than the mother.

Life went on happily enough until one day late in August when I bought an evening paper and on the front page was a picture of our Prime Minister promising 'Peace in our Time'. I felt almost as depressed as on my second journey to Montana. Even Mrs Culver's idiot son knew that it was only Peace for a Time, and that Lucille La Vern on our journey to Southsea might have found proper use for that piece of paper waved by our Prime Minister.

Nevertheless, one can't be forever depressed by the antics of statesmen or, apart from 'Peace in our Time' we would never have any 'Fun in our Time'. So life went on, laughter prevailed, and *French Without Tears* continued until May 1939, when we finally closed. I think some, if not all, of the original cast attended a party on the last night celebrating two and a half years of laughter.

I think all the cast have remained good friends since those days. I was never very intimate with Trevor Howard during the run, he was not exactly in my age group, being sixteen years younger. But since then we are always happy to meet, although I regret that we have never appeared in another play or film together.

CHAPTER X

Success and War

Almost immediately after the run of *French Without Tears*, I started work on the film which was made at Shepperton Studios. Tony Asquith directed and a splendid job he made of it. David Lean was the cutter. I don't believe that the 'cutter' had in those days been elevated to the more dignified title of 'editor'.

Two up-and-coming Hollywood names were engaged to play Katie's and Rex's parts, Ellen Drew and Ray Milland. Jeanine D'Arcy, a pretty little French actress, played the French daughter of the *Patron*, played by a Belgian actor. David Tree, a dear, funny boy, played Kit, Bobby Flemyng's original part.

Whilst I was filming *French Without Tears*, Daphne took a couple of weeks' holiday with one Kil Keen, a darling person and Connie's, my agent's, invaluable secretary, in the South of France. I don't know what these two girls got up to in the Mediterranean sun, but they had a good time together. However, what is sauce for the goose, etc.; when the film finished I took a lone holiday in the same blue skies and also had a good time. Indeed, I have to confess to being unfaithful to Daphne during this holiday. Since I admitted this infidelity to her when I returned home and all her friends soon heard of it, I am sure she will not be concerned if I now tell the story of this short Mediterranean romance.

I was staying at a small pension named La Cigale on the *plage* at St Raphael, recommended to me for its restaurant's superlative cuisine. Here an English couple introduced themselves to me and they in turn introduced me to a most attractive blonde girl, not English but European. She spoke very good English with a slight but attractive accent. Her name was not Marina, but Marina must do for this story. She was staying in a little hotel outside Agay named Le Calangue d'Or about seven miles from St Raphael. She seemed to have plenty of money, but I learnt little of her background or why this very attractive twenty-three-year-old blonde was staying alone on the Côte d'Azur.

The English couple, whose names I fear I have forgotten, Marina and I spent the next several days together, bathing and sunbathing, then lunching and dining at La Cigale. After a day or two it was clear that I was getting a bright green light from Marina. About the third day the four of us took a tame taxi that we had been using to Monte Carlo, lunching (picnic) and a swim on the way, then an afternoon at the Casino gambling. The English couple wished to play roulette for a change, one of the few gambling games that really bore me, but we all played for a while, until suddenly number eleven, on which I had a number of francs, turned up and I had a comfortable win.

Marina immediately said, 'I am bored, Roland, take your nice winnings and buy me a glass of champagne on the terrace.' While we drank our champagne, Marina said perhaps I might care to dine with her at La Calangue d'Or that evening, the other two could drop us there on the way back. I very happily accepted this invitation.

We were duly set down at Marina's charming pub at about 8.30. It was now nearly dark and a crescent moon just rising. The evening seemed promising. I ordered our tame taxi to return for me around midnight. The dinner was excellent and the setting I well remember. The restaurant was on the terrace which, as the name of the hotel suggests, overlooked this beautiful little bay. The scene was pure technicolor, and what's wrong with that? After our coffee and liqueurs we wandered down the terrace steps on to the beach. The moon was now high in the heavens and the stars doing their damnedest to compete with her light. We could hear just the faintest splash of the little ripples on the pebbles. The cigales chirruped away in the conifers behind the hotel. We could also hear the strains of a night-club band about half a mile away, playing a popular romantic number of the time, 'Begin The Beguine'. We kissed. I don't suppose that there is anything particularly original about my lovemaking, so the next few moments I will leave to my readers' imagination.

After a very little while I asked Marina if we could not retire to her room. That, however, was quite out of the question. We would certainly be detected by the *patron* and he would be outraged. So we strolled across the beach out of sight of the hotel and lay down on the pebbles. We discarded our clothes—we didn't have much to discard, she a shirt and shorts, I a shirt and linen trousers. These clothes we bundled up and put under her head for a pillow. The stars were still twinkling, the ripples were still rippling, the cigales were still chirruping and the strains of 'Begin the Beguine' still wafting to us across the bay, and the moon gently lighting up her delightful body. I assumed the traditional position on top of her. Had I been a masochist, the pain of the pebbles digging into my knees and elbows might have enhanced the pleasure of this moment, but I found it abominable torture and the agony quite took the wind from my sails. Not quite the right metaphor, but let it pass. 'Begin the Beguine' sounded louder, but I was not in a position to begin.

But Marina was also in trouble and in a very few moments cried, 'Oh, my darling Roland, you can't do it, you are in too much pebble pain.'

To which I said with true British understatement, 'Well, I do find it a bit uncomfortable.'

Marina said, 'Uncomfortable! More for me too, I have, I think, what you call a barnacle in my bottom!'

Well, that finished that! Laughter and the extreme discomfort of the beach proved too much for further attempts at cohabitation. We dressed in our crumpled clothes and wandered back towards the hotel where my tame taxi was waiting for me.

Residents of my pub La Cigale had keys to the side door in case of late nights at the Casino and I suggested to Marina that she return with me as there would be no problem about getting to my room. But no, she said, it was too late, tomorrow we would dance at the Casino and then she would come to my room. So that was the pattern of the rest of my holiday and a very pleasant pattern it was.

I did see Marina again in England during the war. She had contrived to escape here before the fall of France. But our affair was over and she was now married.

On my return from this holiday, the war clouds were rapidly gathering. About a week before the declaration of war, which we all realised was inevitable. Daphne and my son Michael, now just over a year old, were evacuated with Harold French's wife and daughter to a country house in Hertfordshire. Michael's nanny, whom we had treasured, had to leave us as she was called up as a qualified Red Cross nurse. I was left alone in Hampstead. As I was on Class G Reserve for the RAF I reported to see if I would be wanted.

However, after a brief medical examination the medical officer said, 'What the hell's happened to your left lung?' I explained why there was very little of it left. I was politely told that I would not be wanted. So, that was that. No job in the theatre, no prospect at that time of any films and not even a job in the service. My immediate future looked very gloomy.

The war started, the black-out descended on us all. The London theatres all closed except, I believe, as they afterwards advertised 'We Never Closed', the Windmill Theatre, which exhibited nudes. Of course, they are old hat now, but at the time quite something. I suppose it cheered somebody up; after all, sexy nude girls are, one supposes, a great raiser of spirits. Do I mean spirits?

After a few weeks of the phoney war, there was still little work for actors. I did an ENSA tour round the army camps and RAF stations. For many years, the Green Room Club had given Sunday night shows called 'Green Room Rags'. This ENSA tour in which I appeared was organised by the Green Room Club Rag Committee. The best sketches from many shows were taken and several members of the Green Room took part, together with several actresses, Renée Gadd being one and Gillian Lind another. Apart from sketches there were songs; we were in fact a concert party. One other actor in this group was Ronald Ward, a great friend of mine and a splendid light comedy actor.

This troupe of strolling players would foregather at Drury Lane Theatre at some appointed hour where we took a charabanc to whatever camp we were visiting that night. This ENSA tour lasted eight or ten weeks and then we were for various reasons disbanded. On this tour we were allowed, and paid, the princely sum of £10 a week, which did not keep the wolf very far from our doors. Indeed, my bank balance was dwindling at an alarming rate.

About this time some provincial repertory companies started to function and Daphne was offered a job in Nottingham Rep. As it was rather necessary that one of us should earn at least their keep, Daphne accepted. Our baby son, Michael, was left in the care of the family where they had been living. Then my good friend Angela Fox, née Worthington, volunteered to have him at her home in Sussex, where she had two young sons of her own.

While Daphne was in Nottingham, I rehearsed a new play with Coral Browne, which Harold French directed. We tried out in Newcastle and we were, I believe, the first play to open in London since the start of the war. We opened in January at the New Theatre and ran a week. Actually, I think that is all we could have achieved in peacetime but the incident did not cheer us up exactly.

Early in 1940, Father and Mother closed the London house and rented a small house at Lewknor in Bucks. Soon after this I was compelled, for financial reasons, to ask my landlord to release me from my lease of our Hampstead house, which had another two years to run. He was not too happy about this as he was unlikely to find another tenant at this time, but he made a bargain with me that he would keep all my carpets, curtains and all fittings. This I agreed to but retained all my furniture which I put into store. So while Daphne was in Nottingham, I went to live with her mother in Warwick Gardens, near Earls Court, for a while.

For some reason I did not store our silver or my personal records of plays, etc., and other such possessions, with our furniture but packed them in a trunk and Harold French stored them for me in the basement of his mews house. I saw no more of that. Unhappily, Harold's house had a direct hit during the blitz, sadly killing his wife, Phil. Naturally I did not grieve too much for my loss in the tragic circumstances of Phil's death. In any case, everyone was losing something or other at that time, so what were a few photographs and press cuttings, odds and ends and a little silver. One just didn't concern oneself with such trifles.

In 1940 after the flop in London in January, I was becoming very anxious about my career which had seemed to have caught alight, as it were, with *French Without Tears*. Now the damn bombs began to fall and all the London theatres were closed. So that in the middle of the year I was very happy when the provincial theatres were mostly opened and H. M. Tennents, and other managements, sent out touring companies with leading London actors. We were paid on a profit-sharing basis and business was good in most towns so that we managed to draw quite good incomes. Rex Harrison toured with Diana Wynyard and Anton Walbrook in *Design for Living*. I toured in Freddie Lonsdale's comedy *On Approval* with Diana Churchill, Barry K. Barnes and Cathleen Nesbitt.

I was delighted to meet Cathleen. I had seen her give several splendid performances. I think the first was Yasmin in *Hassan*, then I remembered her as Jessica Madras in *The Madras House*, and also as Margaret Fairfield in a revival of *A Bill of Divorcement* and Florence Churchill in *The Constant Nymph*. But I had never, as I recall, seen her in a light comedy of the Lonsdale type. I loved her at once; she was extremely modest about her talent and considering that she was a more experienced actress than I was actor she was most co-operative at rehearsals and would even take suggestions from me as to how to play the scenes. Lonsdale dialogue is always witty and his characters

Gladys Cooper, Ivor
Novello and Phil Monckman
in California.

Greta Gynt and Nan at 750
Napoli Drive. The Riviera
golf course is in the
distance.

With Peggy Ashcroft on a
picnic during *The Deep
Blue Sea*. Photography by
Kenneth More, who must
have been very funny at the
time.

(*Left*) With Janet Leigh and John Justin during *Safari* (*Right*) Myself during the 1950's.

(*Left*) Practising in Barra while filming *Rockets Galore* by Compton Mackenzie (*Right*)
'Where did that come from?' The New York production of *The Little Hut*.

Aren't we all?, my only London direction in my favourite theatre, the Haymarket. The photograph is signed by the cast.

With Yvonne de Carlo and Peter Ustinov in *Hotel Sahara*.

Five Finger Exercise in New York. *From left to right*: Juliet Mills, Brian Bedford, Jessica Tandy, Michael Bryant, myself.

clearly cut. For some readers who may never have seen *On Approval*, I will tell something of the story: Richard Halton, my character, is in love with a very rich woman, Mrs Wislack, Cathleen's part, who turns out to be a selfish and thorough bitch. But in the short scene I propose to quote in the first act, Richard is unaware of his lady's faults, but her riches are somewhat an embarrassment for him as he is far from rich himself. Marriage is being considered in the following dialogue:

Mrs W. Richard, I should tell you. My income is £25,000 a year.
Richard: Many congratulations.
Mrs W: What's yours?
Richard: Mine?
Mrs W: Yes.
Richard: Well—er—sometimes it's up—then again it's down.

Those few lines are typical Lonsdale dialogue. Very easy to speak and very enjoyable for actors to say. Of course, timing is the secret.

Daphne came on this *On Approval* tour with us as stage manager. This engagement started a long association for her with H. M. Tennents. Daphne's repertory job had finished in March 1940, and we had been living in a pub at Boxmoor. We had retrieved our son who, for a short time, lived once more with his parents. However, when the tour started in July, Michael returned to Angela's care in Sussex.

In the last three months of 1940, the provinces got their share of the blitz. In November we were in Liverpool and there was a particularly heavy raid after the play. I had been invited to supper by an old friend of mine, Arthur Warren, who, incidentally, won the scholarship I had hoped for, my first term at RADA. Before entering showbiz, he had been an officer in the Merchant Navy, and was now 'wavy Navy' in command of a corvette which was docked in Liverpool, and I was to sup on board his ship after the show. I had barely got on board when the sirens started to wail and the din of an air-raid commenced. Naturally, Arthur and I ignored this. He gave me an excellent supper, and we gossiped about old days at the Academy. The all-clear sounded somewhere after midnight and soon I said I had better get back lest Daphne became anxious. When we got on deck we looked over Liverpool lit up with dozens of fires. We agreed that I would be very unlikely to find a taxi and would have to walk. I thanked Arthur and wished him luck and went on my way. I am sorry to say that my wishes of good luck were of no avail; his corvette was sunk and he went down with her.

It took me over an hour dodging between the fires, for some roads I would have wished to go down were closed, before I found myself back at our pub. Daphne was wide awake and not too pleased at my late arrival. I explained that it would not have been very sensible to have attempted to walk home when the raid was on. She complained that I shouldn't have gone in the first place. I promised that I would not go out after the show with any other stray pals I might meet on the tour.

A few weeks after this Daphne informed me that she was pregnant. Now *I* was not too pleased. I think I said, 'Good God, what did you want to do that for?' to which she replied, 'I didn't do it, you did it.' Then I said, 'Don't let's split hairs,' she came back at me with, 'That's exactly what you did split.' I know when I'm beaten and did not argue further. But I pointed out that to have another baby during this bloody war was not a very happy notion as we didn't even have a home. She explained gently in that case we would have to find one.

It was agreed between us and Binkie Beaumont that Daphne would leave the play in May, go back to the Boxmoor pub, retrieve our son Michael once more, and while at the pub try and find a furnished house to rent. Her plan worked out and she found her house, also a very nice local girl whom she engaged to come in daily as a nanny for Michael and for the new baby, when it arrived.

At this time I was earning reasonable money on this tour, but the film industry was looking up, and I had lost two good film jobs, which would have been considerably more remunerative than the play. I had told Binkie, when Daphne left, that I would like to leave the cast as I was losing good film jobs, and finally Binkie replaced me.

When I left *On Approval*, I journeyed to Boxmoor, and I well remember Daphne and my son Michael meeting me at the station. Daphne looking very pregnant and extremely smug, having succeeded with all her plans.

Connie had fixed me in a film to be made at Denham Studios, which I was to start work on in ten days or so. Denham was about an hour's drive from Boxmoor and my old car was falling to pieces and quite unreliable. My brother Douglas had a two-litre, drop-head MG, which he had fitted up to run on calor gas. One needed a minimum of petrol to start the motor then switched over to gas as soon as the engine was running. Douglas sold me this car. The one drawback to this motor was that one had to journey to Elstree Caravan Corner to replace empty gas cylinders. Douglas found this too inconvenient, hence the sale to me. I used this MG for the remainder of 1941 and through '42 into '43.

During the next many months, I played in a number of films, mostly at Denham and largely war films, among them *The First of the Few*, Leslie Howard's last picture before he was killed, *Secret Mission*, also another film of Terence Rattigan's, *English Without Tears, One of our Aircraft is Missing*, and many others. But few of my experiences on these films are worth recounting.

On 18th September 1941, my second son, Robin, was born. The occasion was somewhat traumatic for both Daphne and myself. We had not been expecting the arrival of this new infant for another week or more. My car had developed some minor fault and was that night at our garage in Hemel Hempstead. So, I was without transport. Daphne had just retired to bed and I was downstairs when she called out to me that she was in trouble. I ran up to our room, she was getting out of bed and told me that she was afraid that her water had burst. That I knew was an undesirable happening.

'Are you in labour?' I asked her.

'No pain, no,' she cried, 'but I am soaking wet.'

'Get on the sofa,' I said, 'and I'll call the doctor.'

I ran down to the telephone. The exchange answered with this frightening information, 'Sorry, no private calls, exchange reserved for military use only,' and the telephone clicked off. Here was a pretty kettle of poison. There we were, about three miles from the hospital, no motor car and no telephone. Would I have to try all by myself and deliver our new baby? My God, I was frightened.

Then I had a brainwave; I went to the telephone once more. I didn't give the operator a chance to speak, I said, 'Get me the police, it's urgent.' It worked. 'Police, one moment.'

'Hello,' said a voice. 'What is the trouble?'

Said I, 'I want an ambulance at once. My wife is about to give birth and I am all alone and know nothing about it.'

'Address, please' said the voice.

I gave the voice the address and the voice said, 'Ambulance will be with you as soon as possible.' I thanked him and rang off and returned to Daphne. I asked her how she felt.

'Wet,' she replied.

'No pain?' I asked.

'Not a twinge,' she said. I of course explained that an ambulance was on the way. I said, 'what the devil are we going to do if the baby arrives before the ambulance?'

'Don't be an ass, Culver (Daphne always called me Culver), stop
fussing. I'm not in labour yet. Go and get yourself a drink. I'll yell if
the pain starts.'

I went downstairs and poured myself a large whisky. Happily, the
ambulance arrived before Daphne yelled. A nurse and the ambulance
chap came up with me to help Daphne down to her transport. The
nurse said she would telephone me in the morning when I could go to
see the mother and baby. I explained my telephone situation. 'Oh,'
she said, 'that's because of the heavy air-raid in London. The phone
will be back in normal order when it's over.' At this they departed.

The following morning my garage, who had promised to deliver my
repaired motor-car that morning, kept their word. I drove the
mechanic back to the garage and went on to the hospital and
inspected my new son, who looked to me precisely as all new-born
babies do—not nearly as pretty as puppies! Daphne had not had a bad
time and she was looking to me, as most new mothers look on these
occasions, smug and happy, having achieved something that apparently no one, previously, had ever accomplished.

We remained in Boxmoor for just under two years. I worked in films
mainly at Denham Studios. I had the use of my MG until early in
1943, when authority compelled me to switch to a self-drive hired car.
In the winter of 1942/43, I played the same part in the film of *On
Approval* that I had played in the theatre. This with Clive Brook,
Beatrice Lillie and Googie Withers. It turned out to be a very successful film and, indeed, was mainly responsible for my journey to
Hollywood a couple of years later. It had a record run in a Hollywood
cinema of twenty-two weeks.

Early in 1943, when England and the United States were beginning
to achieve some victories over our common enemies instead of the
series of defeats, the bombing of London seemed to be over, and as
Daphne was working again, stage managing for Tennents, our Boxmoor home was somewhat inconvenient and we decided to return to
London. We moved to a very charming and roomy flat at the summit
of Hampstead Heath, in a block named Bellmore. This we had to
carpet and curtain, and retrieve all our furniture from store and add to
it.

Whilst working for Binkie, Daphne had become a kind of talent
scout, as well as stage manager, and she took a young actor who she
thought had enormous promise under her wing. He came to live with
us at Bellmore. Richard Burton was the chap. Daphne had an eye for
talent. Richard lived with us on and off until he joined the Air Force,

some time in 1944. While he was living with us he had his first great
success in London at the St Martin's Theatre in Emlyn Williams' *The
Druid's Rest*. I did not see much of him at Bellmore as I was working
most of the time. But I do remember Daphne and I took him with us
for drinks one evening with the Clive Brooks and he was very thrilled
to meet Clive. The Brooks at this time lived in a charming house in
Hampstead within walking distance from Bellmore.

Daphne remained a firm friend of Richard's for some years. When I
was in Hollywood and parted from Daphne she left Bellmore and
moved to a house in Pelham Crescent and Richard occupied the top
floor. It was from this house that Richard married his first wife, Sybil
Williams. Daphne organised the reception for him. I am sorry to say
that since his international successes and wife switches, Daphne has
quite lost touch with him, which is sad for her, because although she
lost a husband, she is not in the habit of losing friends.

CHAPTER XI

An Ideal Husband

In late September 1943, an old friend of mine, Jack Minster, asked me if I would like to appear in the play *An Ideal Husband* by Oscar Wilde, which he was going to direct. Rex Whistler was to be the costume designer and scenic artist, and the production, Jack promised me, would be quite beautiful. He had seen the designs. I told Jack I would read the play and asked him to give me a few days to think it over. I read it and decided at once. The production was at the Westminster Theatre.

At the first rehearsal I knew most of the cast. Martita Hunt I knew well, but had never worked with her. Irene Vanbrugh I had acted with eighteen years earlier. Esme Percy had directed me in *The Likes of Her*. Manning Wiley I had played with in a war picture earlier in the war.

I said to Jack, 'Who's the beautiful blonde in the large hat?'

'Nan Hopkins,' said Jack.

She is now Nan Culver. I did not marry Nan until 1947 and I do not propose to go into the ramifications of divorce from Daphne, or apportion blame. Quite clearly, the blame was mine. We will leave it at that.

An Ideal Husband was quite the most beautifully staged production in which I have ever appeared. In exquisite taste. Each of the women's dresses was correct for character and faultless in period, and utterly lovely. The sets were equally enchanting. Elegant, colourful and never vulgar. Unhappily, it was Rex Whistler's last contribution to the London theatre. He was killed in France not long after D-Day. A great loss.

Irene Vanbrugh at this time was a fairly old lady and was beginning to have some difficulty in remembering her lines, and on occasions the other characters on the stage with her became somewhat nervous. Nevertheless, she rose above her handicap and gave a charming performance.

Martita played Mrs Cheveley, the naughty lady of the play. I had a long scene with her in the third act as Lord Goring. For some reason I could not understand, Rex Whistler, in my opinion, made his only mistake in the production—he topped her with a hideous red wig. Now Martita had a strong and charming personality but no one, I think, could describe her as a beauty, and in spite of her entrancing gowns, she contrived with this red wig to look to me like the Widow Twankey. None the less, she gave a splendid performance and it didn't seem to matter. Martita, like me, was a gambler and during the intervals we would sometimes go through the form book together and see if we could find a certainty for the next day's race meeting.

Nan was playing a small part in the opening scene of the play, looking lovely of course, but she was pretty bored that she was not playing a better part for at this time she was quite an ambitious actress.

I adored my part; it was packed with Wilde wit and except for one comparatively serious scene with Lady Chilton in the last act it sparkled with comedy even in the somewhat dramatic scene with Martita in the third act.

The play was an immediate success and we played to packed houses from November to February, when business fell off temporarily when we had a short, but very sharp, blitz once again. So violent did it seem that my sons were once more evacuated, this time with their new nanny to my parents' little house at Lewknor.

Although business dropped off somewhat during the February blitz, by this stage of the war Londoners were so used to air-raids that this occasion did not by any means empty the theatres. However, some evenings were very noisy indeed.

This blitz lasted, perhaps, two or three weeks, then once again all was quiet over London, and the theatre filled up until June; then came the doodlebugs. They were much more unpleasant than ordinary air-raids and as the attack on London by these beastly things intensified, they did succeed in emptying the theatres.

An Ideal Husband closed in London, and we went on a tour of the provinces. Martita Hunt did not choose to go on this tour and Nan, my present wife, who had been understudying Martita, took over the part. Nan was considerably younger than Martita, and obviously less experienced, but she gave a splendid performance and looked exquisitely beautiful in these glorious Rex Whistler gowns.

We finished the tour at the end of August and I returned home to Bellmore. In September, Binkie asked me to play in a new Freddie Lonsdale play entitled *Another Love Story*—a rather appropriate title for my situation at that time. I agreed to do this. The cast was to be Anton Walbrook, Zena Dare, Judy Campbell and A. E. Matthews. We rehearsed in September/October and toured the play in November, opening at the Phoenix Theatre in London in December. During rehearsals, the V2 rockets had started to fall on London. They were not nearly so disturbing as the doodlebugs, since one could not spend the whole day and night anticipating death or injury. These V2 explosions continued nightly during the run of the play.

I had met Zena Dare before but never acted with her. She was a picture postcard pin-up in my youth as was her sister Phyllis. She was delightful to work with. I had a three-handed scene with her and Mattie in the first act, when she battled splendidly for me against Mattie's tricks, which I will come to later. My character is something of an ass in the play, but rich; he has foolishly compromised himself with a designing girl who claims she is going to have his baby. He is however in love with another girl. The dialogue in this scene goes something like this:

Mattie: You would seem to be in something of a dilemma, old fella.
Zena: If you don't like the girl, why did you have an affair in the first place?
My part: It wasn't really an affair.
Mattie: But you say she says she is pregnant and you are the chap.
My part: Yes. Well you see. I was a house guest and we were alone. Her parents had gone to church.
Zena: A Sunday, was it?
My part: Yes.
Zena: Oh! Well, the better the day the better the deed.
Mattie: But why did you do it?
My part: I couldn't think of anything to talk about.

This scene went on for perhaps five minutes. Most of the laughs in it should have been mine, but the only feed lines from Mattie were said either on the floor or when wiping his nose. Not very helpful.

Another Love Story was only a partial success and we ran until March. I had an amusing part and much of it I enjoyed. Freddie's dialogue and characterisation were always fun. However, I mentioned earlier although I liked the wicked fellow Mattie away from the theatre, he was hell to act with. He really could see no reason why anyone should get a laugh from the audience except himself while he was on stage. I don't propose to tell the whole plot of this play, suffice it that in the last act my character was in a somewhat confused state of mind. This following line may not seem particularly funny, but in the situation of the play it was. Mattie was reclining on a settee on the far side of the stage to the door in which I made an entrance. I entered very glumly and remained at the door looking at him. All he has to say is, 'No, go.' Well, he couldn't very well muff that. I replied, 'If the most respectable woman in the world came into this room now, without a stitch of clothing on, I should be able to say to her with the deepest sincerity, Madame, you do not surprise me.'

This speech received a howl of laughter. During my delivery of this line, Mattie on the other side of the stage would get up to his tricks. Out would come his handkerchief, blow his nose. Uncross his legs, bend down and do up his shoelaces, etc, etc. But whatever he might contrive to think up to distract the attention of the audience, still the laugh came. One night in the wings, he said to me, 'Roly, what the hell is funny about that line. Not funny to me.'

This was the occasion when I said, 'Mattie, you are without exception the most selfish actor I have ever met. Come and have a drink in my room and I will go into the technique of comedy with you. God knows you should have learned it by now. What age are you, coming up eighty?' He only laughed.

By now the end of the war was approaching, but so also was the end of our marriage.

About February of 1945, Nan went to Holland, Belgium and France with an ENSA tour entertaining the troops, as I was to do later. Our affair had, of course, started, but as yet divorce had not been settled. Daphne was aware of the situation but was not very grieved as she was, herself, in love with another chap. And who is to blame her? Through much of the war I was seldom home until one or two o'clock in the morning. When not filming, when I had to be up betimes, I would be at the green baize either at Bate's Club in Tilney Street, or Crockford's in Carlton House Terrace, playing poker. Sometimes losing two or three hundred pounds or more, and sometimes winning it. This gambling bug of mine certainly did not contribute to a tranquil marriage; neither when married to Nan did it help our marriage along in the smoothest possible way. We had a charming mews house, now sadly pulled down, in Carlton Mews, our front door being perhaps one hundred yards from Crockford's. The devil only had to reach out his hand, grab my arm as I approached our house and drag me into the club. Nan, however, had a more determined way with the devil than had Daphne, and finally succeeded in amputating his grabbing fingers. But she had a struggle.

I no longer have the desire to gamble for high stakes. My card playing these days consists of bridge at the Garrick and Green Room Clubs, for stakes which I would once have considered peanuts. Horses I had given my best long since. Nowadays, I am somewhat ashamed to admit to some of my past racing friends that I hardly know a plater from a classic horse.

In the early spring of 1945, after the run of *Another Love Story*, I acted in a film *Perfect Strangers*, with Robert Donat, Deborah Kerr, Ann Todd and Glynis Johns. Alexander Korda directed and much of it was shot on location in Scotland at Dunoon. I was the chap who didn't get the girl! Well, I suppose I could hardly expect to with that handsome fella Donat around. I don't remember much about it except that I had a scene with Deborah on the downs overlooking Loch Long, and I had considerable toupee trouble as there was a strong breeze blowing. At one point, after spending a couple of hours arranging my hair, Alex thought it might be a good idea if I wore a hat. But the wind must have dropped, I think, as I am sure I finished the scene without a hat. There were many laughs at my expense but I am used to that. Deborah was a dear to work with.

By 1945 Daphne had worked herself into an important position in the Tennent management. She also arranged several productions through Binkie for ENSA. The European war was over and Binkie suggested to Daphne that it would be a good idea, as Rex Harrison and I were not at that moment working, if we did an ENSA tour of *French Without Tears* on the Continent, with Anna Neagle. We were all rather older than Terence Rattigan's description of the characters, but it didn't seem to matter. Daphne was manager-cum-director, and considered herself, no doubt quite rightly, a pretty important person.

Once in our ENSA uniforms she became, if she will forgive the comparison, a kind of regimental sergeant-major. The company flew to Eindhoven in Holland where we started our tour. After visiting several towns in Holland and Belgium we arrived in Brussels. There before lunchtime on the Friday I was at the bar having a drink with

Rex, when a page handed me a telegram which read, 'Can arrange excellent Hollywood contract Paramount Pictures Olivia de Havilland starring. ENSA will release you. Would require you flying London from Paris Tuesday. Fly New York weekend. Reply return. If yes Paramount representative will contact you in Paris on Monday. Connie.'

'Read that,' I said to Rex.

Rex read.

'Well, I'll be damned!' said he. 'Of course you won't do it.'

'Not do it?' said I. 'Of course I shall do it.'

Said Rex, 'But damn it, old man, you can't do that, old man. You can't leave me all alone with an understudy. And what about the troops?'

I said, 'Well there are only another ten days of the tour left, I daresay the troops will be content with you and Anna.'

Said Rex, 'If I may say so, dear boy, your attitude is that of the shit which you undoubtedly are.'

'Maybe you have a point,' said I. 'None the less, I am afraid I intend to live up to or down to your opinion. After all, it is my career.'

'Your career,' answered Harrison. 'What's the matter with your career? You are in demand in the London theatre; you get plenty of films. What do you want to go to Hollywood for? It's finished, old man; last legs, dear boy. You are making a big mistake. Take it from me, Hollywood's had it. Besides, you haven't even read the script. May be a lousy part and a rotten picture.'

Said I, 'It seems to me improbable that Paramount would go to the trouble and expense of lugging me away from Paris and flying me to California for a lousy picture and a bad part. Anyway, obviously from Connie's wire it's bloody good money.'

'May be,' said Rex, 'and if you earn too much of it you can pay a hell of a lot to the Inland Revenue or spend too much and get into a bugger's muddle with your tax. You realise, of course, that you will have to pay both ends, U.S. tax and English. You'll probably finish up with bugger all.'

'I'll take a chance on that. Excuse me, I had better go and answer this wire. Fill your glass up on me, chum, and order me one.'

I left him at the bar and sent these four words to Connie: 'The answer is yes.'

I then returned to the bar and Rex, who had recovered his good humour, 'Well, good luck in Hollywood, but don't say I didn't warn you. It's old hat, old man.'

I flew to Hollywood, then back home, and returned to Hollywood in February. The first Englishman I saw propping up the bar of that famous pub Romanoff's was Rex!

Now to return to Brussels and my subsequent adventures. We flew to Paris on Sunday morning and got settled into our hotel by lunchtime. I don't remember clearly the Sunday evening. I know Rex and I met Carol Reed who was in Paris at the time and we three went on the town.

On the Monday morning I was not feeling in very good shape. At ten o'clock there was a knock on my door and a page announced that a Paramount *Monsieur* wished to see me. I had not expected such an early call from Paramount. However, I had just bathed so flung on my clothes and went down to meet the chap. I don't think I looked my best; the fellow may well have wondered why his masters in Hollywood were so anxious for my services! But he was a tactful soul and made no unkind cracks.

We proceeded by cab to the Place Vendome to collect a priority flight ticket to London for the following day. I was instructed by my mentor that on arrival in London I should go straight to the Paramount office and ask for Mr David Rose, who from then on would take care of me. But on Tuesday, in Paris, the weather prevented any flights to London and I saw Hollywood vanishing into the mists, so I played in the theatre again that night.

Waking on Wednesday and looking out of my window visibility did not seem much improved. However, the Paramount chap collected me and we were driven to the airport. I boarded a Dakota about midday and was flown to Croydon. As we took off I hoped that the pilot could see further than I could!

At Croydon I found an agitated Paramount representative waiting for me, and I was driven straight up to the Paramount offices in London where I met Mr Rose, who proved to be a charming American and had everything sorted out. Thursday morning I saw my parents and said *au revoir*. I failed to report the break-up of my marriage to my parents that day as I knew that it would distress my mother. I took a cowardly decision to write at a later date.

At 6.45 am on the Saturday the Paramount boss saw me off on the bus with my fellow passengers, and we headed for Croydon Airport again. Here we boarded a Douglas DC–3 for Shannon in Ireland where we remained until about midday when we boarded another bus and drove to Foynes to board our Boeing 314A Pan American Clipper Flying Boat to New York.

For those of my readers, and I have no doubt there are many, who have never flown in a Pan Am Flying Boat across the Atlantic, I have to tell them that they have missed a very pleasant experience though truly they used to take many hours longer than the modern aeroplane. These aircraft would carry thirty-five passengers across the Atlantic at a cruising speed of 145 mph. Passengers had several separate compartments to choose from, all proportioned like drawing-rooms, which included a fourteen-seat dining-room where meals were served for three hours and first come first served. There was also a bar. All passengers had sleeping berths and were looked after by a flying crew of seven and two stewards.

When safely airborne at about 7.30 pm, several passengers, I among them, journeyed to the bar, where I stayed rather too long but finally with several convivial companions made my way to the dining-room, where we supped and wined very well indeed and it became an extremely gay party—I use the word gay not in its homosexual sense, indeed far from it, as I have an idea that one or two characters of opposite sexes contrived to finish the evening in the wrong berth. But I did not go that far myself—I don't think I had such an invitation.

The flight was scheduled to refuel at Bothwood in Newfoundland, which took sixteen hours from Foynes in Ireland. Owing to adverse weather conditions we were diverted to Halifax, Nova Scotia, which added about an hour to our first stop. Here all the passengers disembarked whilst the aircraft refuelled, but we were told by the captain that the weather was too bad to continue our flight that day and we would all have to stay the night at an hotel in Halifax. We arrived at the hotel about 1 pm Canadian time, and lunched. Before we did so one of our convivial bar companions made a hideous discovery. Halifax was 'dry' on Sundays. Not a drink to be had. We all resigned ourselves to this rather tiresome situation, and after lunch, for the rest of the afternoon, I played bridge with three other passengers.

I was not strictly accurate when I maintain that we all resigned ourselves to this 'dry' Sunday. Our convivial friend by no means accepted such resignation, and at about 5.30 he strolled into the lounge, where we were at our bridge game, with a large parcel under his arm, and a triumphant, self-satisfied grin on his face, and invited any passengers who might be feeling thirsty to his room, first going to their own rooms to collect their tooth-mugs. A number of us accepted this invitation, indeed, all those that were in the lounge at the time. Where he had nosed out the stuff, he did not reveal, but when we arrived in his room there, displayed on his dressing-room table, were three bottles of scotch. A truly remarkable achievement, we thought, since the chap had never been in the town before.

The weather report in the morning was good and we took off for New York at about 7 am. At around 11 I saw New York's famous Statue of Liberty from the air, then a few moments later we docked. I was met by a Paramount representative and driven to the Sherry Netherland Hotel, where I was conducted to an enormous suite overlooking Central Park, given $500 in cash, my weekly expenses allowance, theatre tickets for three Broadway shows and told to enjoy New York for three days. I would be flying to California on the Thursday, Paramount would pay my New York hotel bill. All this sounded rather jolly.

After luncheon I was still feeling a bit jaded after my journey and decided that it would be a good idea, if I was to enjoy my evening, to return to my suite and bed for a few hours. So I had a bath, tucked myself up and was soon asleep.

It would seem that the best laid schemes of mice and men, even Paramount men, 'gang aft a-gley'.

I was wakened at five o'clock by telephone, and told that Paramount wished to see me, and was on his way up. I had a quick wash and donned a dressing-gown. A knock on the door, and Paramount appeared. The Japanese war was still on at this time, and a military order had just been issued that all passengers flights to the West Coast must be cancelled—all flights must be reserved for the forces until further notice. Paramount were most apologetic but the studio wanted me in Hollywood that week so they feared that they were obliged to change all the plans. I was now booked to travel by train that evening, leaving on the Twentieth Century train from Grand Central Station at 8, which would take me to Chicago, where I would be met by another Paramount representative who would entertain me to luncheon at the famous Pump Room. There would be ample time for this as The Chief, the train which would transport me from Chicago to Los Angeles, did not depart for several hours after my arrival on the Twentieth Century. So vanished my three days of fun in New York. I left that evening as arranged.

Everything now went according to Paramount plan. I duly arrived in Chicago, lunched at the Pump Room, and boarded The Chief. My luggage I found neatly stacked in my compartment and a delightful coloured steward looked after all my wants.

When I finally arrived at Los Angeles station, I was met by a publicity gent who escorted me straight to the studios. This was about a half-hour's drive from the station, during which my new Paramount friend explained that Hollywood and Beverly Hills were packed solid owing to the military, and that there was an order in force at the moment that visitors could not occupy any room for more than five days. He also informed me that as yet he did not know if I had any accommodation at all, but hoped and expected that my patron and producer, one Charles Brackett, would have arranged something by the time I had met him at his office.

We arrived at Charles Brackett's office to be informed by his secretary that he was at lunch at Lucy's, a restaurant across the avenue from the studio, and would my publicity friend take me across to join Mr Brackett for luncheon. We dumped my luggage in his office and crossed over to Lucy's. Here I at once spotted several famous faces. Dorothy Lamour was, I remember, the first one I picked out, from mostly Paramount contract stars.

My first impression of Hollywood was more or less as I had imagined, one had read so much about it and seen so many exteriors of Beverly Hills on the screen. I remember my first unpleasant impression was the heat. It was late June and sweat rolled off me in streams. How would I be able to work in this temperature? My toupee would surely float off.

Charles Brackett was a very charming, grey-haired, grey-moustached New Englander, of perhaps fifty-five. He was delighted to welcome me to Hollywood and was most happy that Paramount had been able to obtain my services to play in the film he had written and was producing. He was most apologetic about the accommodation situation. However, he had procured a room for me for the first five days at the Bel Air Bay club, where he would escort me later in the afternoon. After I had settled in he would send a car for me and we would dine together at Romanoffs in Beverly Hills. He explained that it would be quite impossible to get around without a car of my own, and he had arranged with my agent that I should have a driving test next day for a Californian driving licence. I would then hire a self-drive car and be independent.

After lunch, he took me back to the studio and on the set where they were shooting, the film had been in production for several weeks, and introduced me to Olivia de Havilland, looking very beautiful. I was to play practically all my scenes with her when the time came. When the time came! Although they had rushed me away from the pleasures of New York so hastily, I did not start work on that picture for over a month. He also introduced me to Mitch Leisen, the director, and John Lund, the juvenile leading man. John and his charming wife Marie still exchange Christmas cards with us each year, as we also did with Charlie Brackett until his death.

After these introductions, Charlie drove me to the Bel Air Bay Club, which stood high up on a cliff overlooking Santa Monica. I had a delightful, large airy room and bathroom, french windows and a balcony with a view over the Pacific Ocean. Charlie left me saying that he would send a car for me at 8 to take me to dinner.

My car duly picked me up and drove me to Romanoffs, where I again saw many famous faces. The first I recognised was an actor I had known in England, Herbert Marshall, with his wife occupying a corner table near the entrance. I was to learn that they dined at that table most evenings. Charlie was waiting for me and walking down the restaurant to our table, among others he discreetly pointed out to me Hedda Hopper, the columnist.

I am seldom able to remember a woman's clothes on any particular occasion, a failing that is apt to irritate Nan whose main interest in life, after me, is fashion. 'What was so and so wearing?' she will ask. 'I haven't a clue,' I will reply. 'Oh, you are infuriating, you must have some clue. What colour was her dress?' 'Darling, there were so many women there and many I noticed were wearing a similar colour.' 'Well, what colour was that?' 'Pink,' I might say, 'or was it red? No, come to think of it it was green—or was it?' 'Oh, you are hopeless, darling, pour me a drink.'

In spite of this mental defect of mine, I do happen to remember well Hedda Hopper's display that evening. She was wearing daffodil yellow. She was also wearing a headdress that I think perhaps was intended to resemble a daffodil. She was quite conspicuous and had Charlie not pointed her out I should probably have asked him who she was. Actually I think that Hedda Hopper was the only daffodil I ever saw in California. They don't take kindly to the climate.

Romanoffs was the equivalent to the Savoy Grill or the Ivy Restaurant in London before and during the war. Actors and actresses abounded. Beautiful women littered the place. Hollywood, of course, was a magnet for young pretty girls hoping to get a chance on the silver screen. Many of them did not get that chance but many found an escort, perhaps an agent, to take them to dinner at

Romanoffs. So that all the glamour was not confined to the film stars, but of course there were quite a few of them there.

Mike Romanoff himself was a nice, quiet-spoken little man and an excellent restaurateur. Whether he was of royal Romanoff blood is in some doubt. I don't believe that he ever claimed that the blue fluid ran through his veins; on the other hand he never denied the rumour as far as I know.

I noticed a number of famous faces during that dinner with Charlie, but as I begin to remember who they were, I realise that more than half of them are dead, including Charlie himself. If I want to finish this story, I'd better get cracking before I see them all again in one place or the other.

CHAPTER XII

Tinsel Town

When I left Charlie I was driven back to my temporary quarters. I was very tired and was in bed and asleep in a very few minutes. I awakened about 8, drew my curtains to look out at a clear sunny day, and completely calm blue sea, and was fascinated to watch the pelicans diving for their breakfast in that millpond ocean. They would perch on a breakwater and then fly up, perhaps fifty feet above the water, then dive with a great splash and presumably come up with a beak full of fish, then they would continue their flight to the next breakwater, where they would rest for a moment and repeat the performance back to the original perch. Sometimes they would stay paddling around where they had flopped in before taking off again. I watched this entertaining performance for several minutes before deciding to shave, bathe and dress, which I managed to do before breakfast arrived.

At about 10.30 a studio car came to take me to my agent in Beverly Hills. Frank Vincent was the agency and a chap named Tom Somlio, his active partner, was to look after my affairs. Cary Grant was, incidentally, a sleeping partner in the Vincent Agency. Tom Somlio took me to have my driving test and I achieved my licence by midday; I then hired a car and became independent. Tom Somlio was very pleasant and was most helpful in putting me wise to the ways of Tinsel Town. He also asked me if I played golf. I told him I used to play continually and had once had a stage-golfing handicap of nine before the war. But I explained that I had no opportunity at all to play during the war—in other words, I hadn't handled a golf club for six years and I suspected that I had quite lost my swing. Tom suggested that I should go to one of the several driving ranges round about Hollywood and Beverly Hills, buy a set of new clubs, practise, and see what my swing was like. This I did, and as I had suspected, my swing had left me completely. I simply could not hit a ball; I might have been a spastic so little did my muscles co-ordinate. Nevertheless, I continued to slash away at these driving ranges. This was, of course, the wrong way to go to work, I should have visited a good pro who would have taken my swing to pieces and put it correctly together again. This lack of golfing ability was to prove an embarrassment and an annoyance the following year when I journeyed to Canada in a film with Bing.

During my first week I was invited to several parties. The first was to Nigel Bruce's house. Nigel Bruce, known as Willie, I knew in England. This was quite a small dinner party and among the guests, one most anxious to meet me was Freddie Lonsdale, whose *On Approval* had been such a success in Hollywood. He turned out to be a big fan of mine and we became very good friends. Willie and I also became chums and eighteen months or so later, when I was once more playing respectable golf, he and I would play at our club, The Riviera, almost daily, when neither of us were working.

Freddie Lonsdale was a very amusing man with a tremendous personality and a very quiet voice. If there was a hubbub of conversation he would never attempt to butt in or top one of the noisy members of the party; should he wish to gain the attention of the assembled company he would sit very still yet somehow be very conspicuous and one would notice him gently tweaking the end of his long nose between his finger and thumb. Suddenly there would be silence and then in his soft voice he would make some witty remark, probably at the expense of one of the noisier guests.

The First Sunday after my arrival, Charlie Brackett gave a large luncheon party for me at his house in Bel Air. As by this time I had been, so to speak, 'expelled' from the Bel Air Bay Club, I was now staying at the Bel Air Hotel, which was only two or three minutes' walk from Charlie's house. I had been warned by Tom Somlio never to arrive at a large party less than half an hour or more after the time of the invitation. A very good tip. At an evening party he suggested that an hour late, at least, was advisable, as there was still liable to be two hours' drinking before dinner was served, and abstinence prior to one's advent was a wise restraint.

On the Sunday of Charlie's party, I walked round to the house half an hour late as advised. Even so, when greeted by Charles's charming and very amusing wife, Elizabeth, there were only about half a dozen guests ahead of me. John Lund and Marie were one couple, so that was a help. During the next half-hour, the place began to fill up.

Hedda Hopper arrived and once again I remember her get-up. She wore a flowing silk dress of a similar colour to the one I had first seen her in at Romanoffs. It may seem odd with my apparent lack of interest in the apparel of chance women acquaintances that I should remember Miss Hopper's on two occasions. The fact is that this occasion was, even for me, quite unforgettable. The *pièce de résistance* being a solid gold hat, plaited gold strips designed like a straw boater, with a gold mesh veil. This hat, needless to say, was discussed by all and sundry, as indeed it was expected to be. Whether it was actually admired by the other members of her sex, I would not venture to surmise. I should have thought that it was extremely heavy, and, as it was a very hot day, somewhat uncomfortable. However, Hedda Hopper was famous for her hats, so I suppose that I should have felt honoured that she wore her gold one to meet me.

During my first stay in Hollywood, Hedda Hopper and Louella Parsons, but particularly Hedda, gave me a lot of praiseful publicity. However, I cooked my goose with those ladies as at this time I was in the throes of divorce and I did not let on until it was a *fait accompli*, over a year later when it was no longer scandal news. I had no intention of letting my parents hear of my broken marriage through a gossip column. The columnist ladies did not forgive me for my selfish secrecy. Divorce intrigue is public property, particularly if you are a Hollywood actor. Columnists have a divine right to relevant information.

There were several well-known stars at Charlie Brackett's luncheon, but as I met most of the current stars from time to time at various parties, I fear that now I can't remember whom I met where. I was invited to a large party at Ronald Colman's. Benita Hume, his wife, I had met in London years before, and she was fun, and although I never became very keen on the big Hollywood parties, I enjoyed myself that evening.

The second party I attended at the Colmans was disastrous and very embarrassing. I made a social blot. I became locked in the lavatory. Having had a pee, which I badly needed, I started on the key of the door. I fiddled and tweedled, twisted and wriggled but was unable to get the damned door unlocked. The room was on the ground floor, so it occurred to me that the obvious thing to do was to climb out of the window. Then I did a very foolish thing; I had had rather a lot to drink, and out in the fresh air I decided that it would be prudent to drive home while I was capable of driving. So without more ado, without a thank you or good-night to my host and hostess or any explanation, I went home.

Next morning I awakened at about 6.30. I was due at the studio at 8.30 and did not have a hangover, but the thought of my horrific ill manners of the previous evening brought me out in a cold sweat. Immediately I sat down and wrote a letter of apology to Benita. I then went to the studio. One night some six or seven weeks later when I retrieved a bottle of whisky—which readers will hear of later—from the glove compartment of my car I found tucked at the back of the cubby-hole my letter to Benita. I had forgotten to post it. How it could be that I hadn't discovered it before, I can't say. But it was now too late to write further apology and excuse. Sad, but I never met the Colmans again.

Ronald Colman was, of course, uncrowned King of the English colony and C. Aubrey Smith, Prime Minister, or was it t'other way round? Aubrey ran the cricket team and they attempted to drag me into this. However, my cricket had not improved since my prep schooldays. I think I only appeared once on the Hollywood field; they didn't bother to ask me again.

During my third week in California, I had a most traumatic experience. I was on my last day in my third residence, a motel on Santa Monica Boulevard. I was booked the following day for five days at the Beverly Hills Hotel. Instead, I found myself in Cedars of Lebanon Hospital. In the morning, I journeyed to the studio to have a toupee fitting. I had been irritated the previous evening by a pricking sensation under my tongue, not too painful, but as though a small pip of some kind had lodged there.

On this morning it had become rather more irritating, and after my toupee fitting I visited Charlie Brackett in his office and suggested that perhaps I should see a doctor. He didn't think that necessary and sent me along to the studio first aid room. He thought it was a small pimple that the nurse there could cope with. The nurse looked at it and maintained that perhaps it was worth cauterising. This she did. It was the wrong treatment. She managed to seal up a saliva gland under my tongue.

By the evening I was in quite a lot of pain. I managed after a few drinks to eat something soft for dinner, had a couple more whiskies and three aspirins and got into my motel bed, hoping in the morning that I might be out of pain. I passed out for a few hours but awakened before dawn in considerable pain, with my tongue now extremely swollen. At around 8 I packed, paid my motel bill and drove to the studio, hoping to find someone to help me get a doctor. I managed to drink a cup of tea in the canteen, but did not see Charlie until after 9, when he arrived at his office. By this time, I could scarcely talk. My tongue nearly filled my mouth. Naturally Charlie was desperately concerned and contacted his doctor who said he would see me at once in his surgery.

Arriving at the doctor's, he took one look at my tongue and said I had an abscess and it was a surgeon's job. He told me to rest in his waiting-room until he could arrange an appointment with his colleague in the same building. After what seemed hours to me, but was possibly only minutes, he escorted me up to the surgeon's apartment. This chap examined my tongue, then told me to remove my jacket. I was sweating freely. He sat me down in something rather like a barber's chair. He then proceeded to strap my wrists to the arms of the chair, strap my head with a strap across my forehead to a headrest; he instructed me to open my mouth, and placed two gags either side of my jaw to keep my mouth open. I then had to stick out my tongue, which he secured by some contraption, and my consultant then held on to this, pulling my tongue tight against my upper lip. Now the surgeon gave my tongue several jabs with a local anaesthetic, after which he operated on this abscess which I had developed. While in that chair, I should think I lost seven or eight pounds in weight. The perspiration flowed off me in rivulets.

When I was finally released from my torture, my tongue was numb with the local anaesthetic, and I was told to retain the gags to hold my teeth apart for two hours lest I should bite my nerveless tongue. Now I must go straight into hospital, partly to recover from the shock, but also for exploratory examinations to try to establish the cause of this sudden blow-up. In hospital I was jabbed night and morning in my bottom with penicillin injections, rather viciously, by a very nasty nurse who, I believe, supposed that I had syphilis. Maybe my doctor had some such idea, for after all the various blood tests and, presumably, after the examination of the pus withdrawn from the abscess, he may well have pronounced me clean to my nurse as she became somewhat kinder.

I began to forget my pain, next day, but was very worried about my future. Would I be able to talk properly? Had Paramount decided to recast the part? They must surely have thought of doing so. Tom Somlio visited me the second evening, and he was as anxious as I was, but as yet, though informed of my indisposition, had no suggestion

from Paramount that they had thought of a replacement. I told Tom
that I had practised talking and that my tongue was healing satisfactorily and that I was convinced that my speech would be back to
normal in a day or two. And so it proved.

Charlie Brackett came to see me, about teatime, on the third day.
He had obviously been reassured by the doctor that I was going to be
perfectly fit. He was most charming and sympathetic, and relieved. I
said that I hoped I had not held up the production. He said not at all,
that they had made but the smallest alteration in the schedule and I
should not be shooting for over a week. So take it easy.

I left the hospital three days later and went to the Beverly Hills
Hotel, where Charlie had managed to rebook me for five days. Six
days in hospital had been my longest stay, so far, in one bed.

However, after the Beverly Hills bed, I was invited by an old friend,
indeed an actor I had worked with nearly twenty years previously, one
George Melville Cooper, to stay as P.G. at his house. I accepted this
invitation very willingly indeed.

Very soon after going to live with George and his wife, I did begin
shooting, and work became more or less concentrated. *To Each His
Own* was a sentimental war story. All my scenes with Olivia, who
incidentally was charming to work with, were set in England during
the war. I was playing an ex-English army officer—no explanation as
to why I was ex since I was only supposed to be my age, forty-five. I
was fire watching with Olivia. I was the boss of this fire watching
squad and for some reason, still not explained, I order an inspection of
the roof—I suppose to see if it is still there—before the incendiary
bombs start to fall. Then by some extrordinary carelessness I fall off,
or nearly do so, but Olivia saves me. I don't think it would be
particularly interesting reading if I recounted all the twists and turns
of this story, suffice it that it was packed with historical inaccuracies
and domestic absurdities: such as the *ingénue*, an officer in the WRNS,
marrying a United States lieutenant, the wedding taking place in the
Savoy Hotel. I ventured to point out that marriage in England invariably took place in either a church or a register office. I had never heard
of a Savoy marriage. No offence was taken at my objections, they were
tolerantly ignored. During the shooting, at the end of each shot, it was
unanimously proclaimed to be 'out of this world'. Everything Olivia
did, indeed, everything I did, was 'out of this world'. It was generally
accepted as a certainty that Olivia would win the Oscar for her
performance, and the film would also get the Oscar. Was not the
whole production 'out of this world'?

These prognostications proved to be uncannily accurate. Olivia got her Oscar, Charlie got his for the script, and I believe several other Oscars were awarded to this very whimsical film. Olivia no doubt deserved her Oscar. Much as I liked Charlie and appreciated his kindness to me, I really cannot accept the opinion that this sentimental little story deserved a gold medal, indeed, very touch and go for a bronze. Nevertheless, I enjoyed myself. It was a very happy cast and all went smoothly. We finished shooting on the last day of my guarantee, but I stayed on in Hollywood for another ten days on expense allowance, in case any retakes were needed.

A week after we had finished shooting, there was a sneak preview at Long Beach, about thirty miles away. It was arranged that I should drive down with Elizabeth Brackett and Zan, their daughter. Charlie was to go with the director and other Paramount executives to enable them to have an immediate private conference after the showing. I was to call for Elizabeth and Zan at their Bel Air house. This I did. Elizabeth decided that since Zan knew the way, it would be best for her to drive us in her car and leave mine at the house.

During the long drive home after the film, in the middle of nowhere amongst a forest of oil derricks, about midnight, Zan's car spluttered and stopped. As far as I am concerned, if a car stops, I know no way of making it go again if kicking fails to have any effect. Very rarely it does. So, there we were. Not a sign of life, nothing on the road, Zan had taken a short-cut. Elizabeth was philosophical. We would just have to wait until another car came along and rescued us. This did not happen for half an hour. Eventually a jeep full of sailors appeared. We waved it to a stop. Now what to do? Should I go with the sailors to get help and leave the two women alone on this deserted road, or let Zan go with the sailors and leave me with Elizabeth. We decided on the latter course.

At this time, scotch whisky was almost in as short supply in Hollywood as in England. But that afternoon I had managed to buy a bottle for $10. It was now resting in the cubby-hole of the dashboard of my car, parked in Charlie's drive. As Zan left us, I said to Elizabeth, 'My God, I should like a drink.'

'So should I,' said Elizabeth.

I then explained to her that I could see quite clearly in my mind's eye, my bottle of scotch nestling in that glove compartment. She roared with laughter. I did not learn until much later that Elizabeth was an alcoholic. In the picture, *Lost Weekend*, the story of an alcoholic, written by Charlie some time later, the drunken character had just such a vision. Elizabeth used to help Charlie when writing his pictures!

Zan eventually returned with a couple of mechanics and we were rescued. We arrived back at the house after two o'clock. Charlie had been very worried indeed, having been home over an hour. He had not taken a short-cut. When I said good-bye to Charlie, he assured me that it was only *au revoir*, and that he wanted me for another picture which he would be making the following spring.

Again I had to journey to New York by train, where after one night I boarded the *Queen Elizabeth*. Five days of relaxed pleasure. Oh dear, why is the world in such a hurry now? After that first voyage, I always crossed to and from the States, whenever I could do so, in a liner. Two more trips in the *Elizabeth*, one in the *Mary*, one in the *Mauretania* and one in the *Liberté*, her last voyage.

I arrived home towards the end of September. Daphne was, once again, on another try-out tour and my two sons were at Bellmore with their nanny. Nan, now parted from her husband, was living with her mother in Hampstead. While I was away, Nan had found this charming Carlton Mews House, but it needed much decorating and some structural alterations made before it was habitable. Indeed, it was not ready until the end of October. Meanwhile, I returned to my flat for some time.

I imagine most divorces are, in some way, distressing to all concerned. Ours was no exception. There must be some heart-searching, also, if one has young children, a feeling of guilt and sorrow. So it was with me. None the less, it was inevitable. But at this time divorce was not all that easy; the courts were brimming over with these cases, and one had to wait one's turn, which in our case was many months.

Before Daphne returned from her tour, I had fixed a film at Welwyn Studios, in which Eric Portman was playing a murderer, and Dulcie Gray, the leading frightened lady. I played the detective. Welwyn is a long drive and I decided that apart from divorce it would be best to stay in a pub at Welwyn during the shooting, until our mews house was ready. Nan and I moved into the mews in November, when my film was over.

I learned from Connie in December that she now had the Paramount contract that Charlie Brackett had promised. It was to play in the film *The Emperor Waltz*, with Bing Crosby and Joan Fontaine starring. This was to be done at the end of April 1946. Then at the beginning of January, Columbia Pictures offered me a contract to play in *Down to Earth*, with Rita Hayworth starring, in February. They were aware that this might overlap a few days with *The Emperor Waltz*, but were prepared to risk that inconvenience.

I arranged with Daphne that my elder son, Michael, should go to Cottesmore Prep School, which Larry Olivier had recommened to Daphne. His son Tarquin was already there. Michael was to go for the summer term of 1946, and Robin, my younger son, eighteen months later. Meanwhile, Daphne lived at Bellmore for a few more months.

Come February, Nan and I were unhappy that she could not accompany me to Hollywood, but since there was not as yet any sign of the divorces getting into court, it was quite impossible to take her with me.

CHAPTER XIII

Nan Joins Me in Hollywood

This time, my journey to California was by air all the way. Tom Somlio met me at the airport. I was to be at Columbia Studios the next morning to meet my producer and director. That evening, as recounted, I went to Romanoffs for dinner where I met Rex.

Rex and Lilli were in a rented house in the heights of Bel Air, naturally, with a swimming pool. Very few houses were *sans* swimming pool.

Down To Earth was a musical sequel to the film *Here Comes Mr Jordan*, in which Claude Rains played Mr Jordan. Now I was to play the same character. I admit to feeling highly flattered to be playing a part that my most respected and admired instructor at RADA had originally created. Having arrived at the studio next day, I met the director and producer, and then went up to the make-up department.

The character, Mr Jordan, was the equivalent to St Peter at the Gates of Heaven, but in this story, Jordan was at the entrance to Mount Parnassus. This character had to wear a snow-white toupee, a kind of halo. This bright hair-piece had to join in, like any other toupee, with my own hair. But my own hair was far from white, so what does this hairdresser-lady do, but dye my hair and turn me into a platinum blonde. Very embarrassing; I looked a proper Charlie. This middle-aged, bald-headed ham, the remainder of whose thatch was obviously dyed.

I started work in *Down to Earth* on the Wednesday of the next week, resplendent in white toupee and blue uniform of Mr Jordan. I had met Rita Hayworth at the studio the previous Thursday. She was very lovely and very pleasant. Early on the Wednesday morning, a studio car drove Rita and me to Sonja Henie's ice rink, where we were to shoot the scenes on Mt Parnassus. Rita was playing one of the nine

muses, Terpsichore, goddess of dancing. The reason for the scenes at
the entrance to Mount Parnassus being shot on Sonja Henie's ice rink
was that dry-ice, powdered solid carbon-dioxide sprayed on to the
rink, remained spread about eight inches above the ice and gave a
realistic effect of clouds on which the immortal characters walked.
Here I stood beside a heavenly aircraft checking the new mortals,
recently dead, who while on earth had lived lives worthy of immortal-
ity on Zeus or Apollo's Mount. This aircraft was to transport these
new immortals on their final journey to the sacred and joyous land.

Among the group of new arrivals was the handsome juvenile leading man. I check him on my passenger list then say, 'There seems to be
some mistake. You are not due here for another two years.' I fear I
have forgotten the reason for his premature presence at Mr Jordan's
checkpoint, I think the medical profession on earth were to blame.
There had been an accident of some kind and he had been pronounced
dead, when only unconscious, but I don't believe they had gone to the
unpleasant procedure of burying him.

During my scene with the young man, where he tried unsuccess-
fully to convince me that he really was dead, Terpsichore, in a gay and
abandoned mood, was dancing all over the Mount and arrived at the
gates. How she was able to arrive there, since an aircraft was needed
to carry the rest of the company to Apollo or Zeus, I really don't think
was explained. However, being a goddess I suppose she was able to
get around the place at will, unlike the hoi polloi. Immediately she
arrived, as I was chatting to the young handsome chap who had no
business to be there, their eyes met and that was that. Love at first
sight and no nonsense. But I fear that before they had a chance to get
into a clinch, he vanished from her sight and woke up on earth, from
where he should never have departed.

Terpsichore was desolated. 'That,' she declared, 'was the chap she
had been waiting for through eternity.' Have him she must. Please
would I plead with Zeus, her papa, to allow her to go down to earth
and grab him before some nasty, scheming, sexy bitch of a mortal
snared him. I did not have a scene with Zeus, pleading for his
love-lorn daughter, as Zeus did not appear in the film. But it was
assumed that I received the okay from the boss to go ahead, as
Terpsichore is next seen dancing as a mortal at a theatre rehearsal and
the young man very close by, while I am standing on one side with a
kindly smirk on my face. Naturally this fantasy ended happily ever
after, oddly enough, two years later when the juvenile was killed, the
pair of them scarpered back to Parnassus; on this occasion I was

happy to let him in. Since Zeus had nine daughters, I suppose on this Grecian Mount, Terpsichore, as other gods and goddesses, was able to have pleasure with her lover other than dancing. I believe another remake of Mr Jordan is now going the rounds entitled *Heaven Can Wait*, but I don't know what Mr Jordan gets up to in this production.

So much for my second picture in Tinsel Town. I had only just completed my work in it when Paramount required my services for *Emperor Waltz*. This necessitated a journey to Jasper National Park in the Canadian Rockies for something over six weeks, the Rockies representing the Austrian Tyrol.

The budget of *Emperor Waltz* must have been prodigious. It was a period musical, set in the Austro-Hungarian Empire of 1900, partly in the court of Franz Joseph and partly in the mountains of the Austrian Tyrol. The costumes were all most elegant, naturally, made for us. I had three uniforms as a General, and Joan Fontaine, my daughter, numerous, very expensive dresses. Bing Crosby's clothes were not quite so expensive, as he was playing an American salesman hawking gramophones around Europe. He did don one Tyrolean outfit, also a dress suit, otherwise he wore men's clothes of the period. Richard Haydn's Franz Joseph, I believe, had two princely outfits. There were several other characters, all immaculate. Then in the final ballroom scene, probably 150 extras dressed up to the nines.

Bing, Joan and myself, and two or three extras, were the only members of the cast who were required in Jasper, but what with a make-up staff of a dozen or more, camera crew, electricians, carpenters, prop men and endless other technicians, it was necessary for Paramount to rent the whole of a hotel and the adjoining bungalows, situated round a beautiful, very blue lake. All the principals had bungalows to themselves, others larger apartment bungalows with separate sleeping quarters. I should suppose that the unit, all told, numbered about 300.

Paramount had been assured that May and June were mainly sunny and fine in the Canadian Rockies. We did not see any sun for the first two weeks. It was continually overcast—no good at all for filming, but very satisfactory for golf. There was a splendid golf course, five minutes' walk from the hotel. This suited Bing down to the ground. He had brought up a friend with him, a scratch golfer, so as to be sure of a good game when not working. I had brought my new set of clubs with me, but stupidly had not as yet had any lessons, believing that I could recover my old swing without them. It was not so, I was still a semi-spastic.

When told on the first morning that there would be no shooting that day, I walked over to the golf club and went on to the practise fairway with a caddie and forty-odd practise balls, and began to slash away. I did connect with the centre of the club but the damn balls never went straight, either a horrible slice to the right or a vicious hook to the left. I had been practising for half an hour when Bing turned up with his pal, and sent his caddie over to me and asked if I would like to make up a four-ball match with him, his pal and the local pro. I joined him and explained that much as I should love a game, I was not in their class as I hadn't played for six years and my swing had deserted me. Bing said it didn't matter as we would handicap accordingly.

So off we went. It was horrible, frustrating and embarrassing. We had to look for my sliced or hooked drive at nearly every hole, and there is nothing more boring for three good players than to play with one bad one, and have their game held up. Not that I allowed anyone to look for my ball for more than a minute, I would say, 'Oh, hell with it, let's get on.' I think I lost eight balls that day. Of course, playing with Bing and that expert company made me more than ordinarily nervous, which didn't help.

Although Bing invited me to play again I refused to spoil their game for the next three weeks while I had concentrated lessons from the assistant pro. He helped me no end and I was able to join up again in games with Bing for the last part of our stay without spoiling the fun.

On days when there seemed some promise of sun and blue sky, the unit would motor off to a location. Bing, Joan and I had a caravan each to dress in. Make-up had a couple of caravans, and Billy Wilder and Charlie had one each. We would arrive at the appointed site where it was hoped we would shoot some scenes. But the clouds were mostly very uncooperative. On these occasions I learnt to my cost a card game new to me, gin rummy. It seemed simple enough and I had seen a couple of chaps play it from time to time, but I had never played it myself. Billy Wilder asked me if I knew the game; I said that I did but had not played it, and he said come and have a game while we are waiting for the sun to shine. I thought the game very simple, and was pretty sure with my card sense, and luck, that I should be able to hold my own. I suppose that Billy relieved me of about $150 or more a week, for the first three or four weeks, waiting for the sun before I began to catch on and hold my own. But only hold my own. I didn't get any of those dollars back. However, I learnt the trick, admittedly the hard way. I frequently played with Joan in her bungalow in the evenings and she beat me at first, but in the end I think we came out about square.

Joan was an entirely different character from her sister, Olivia, more frivolous and a flirt. No offence meant, and I am sure none taken, but we got on very well. For six weeks the weather was unkind to the production; actually, during that time I believe that we only achived five minutes screen time of scenes on film. The only scene I remember having shot was Joan and me in an open carriage, trotting up a mountain road, stopping at a chalet and getting out of the carriage. The one long sequence they managed to get was Bing, in Tyrolean dress, walking up a mountain road singing a number which finished up as a yodelling song with a chorus and Austrian dancing, leg slapping and all that. As far as I recall, that number of Bing's and his final song while dancing with Joan to the tune of *Emperor Waltz* were the only songs in the production. Bing may have had another number at some point, but I fear I don't remember. No one else sang.

During the sixth week, Charlie and Billy surrendered to the weather and took a series of back-projection films when they could grab a bit of blue sky and sunshine, the scenes to be shot over them on our return to the studios. That six weeks, with five minutes film in the can plus back-projection, must have cost, I should suppose, around $700,000 or could be $1,000,000.

During the last week in the Rockies, I talked to Nan on the telephone. In spite of no divorce through as yet, she was now able to join me when I returned to California. Jack Minster, a good friend of us both, had been engaged to direct a production of *Lady Windermere's Fan* for New York, with Cornelia Otis Skinner playing Mrs Erlynne. The rehearsals were to take place in Los Angeles, and the play to open in Santa Barbara, then San Francisco for a month and so on to New York. Jack had convinced the producer that he must have as near as possible an all-English cast, and was able to engage Nan to play a small part.

So Nan arrived in California about three weeks after I had returned from Canada. I met her at Los Angeles airport. We were both very happy to be reunited. Accommodation was still difficult at the time but Jack Minster had managed to rent a furnished house in the heights of Hollywood for the three of us at the very top of Laurel Canyon, where we stayed for the whole of their rehearsal period, over a month. During this time I was of course filming at Paramount.

Nan and Jack left me in the house when they went to Santa Barbara with the play. We had a coloured lady cook-cum-housekeeper whom we retained from the owners of the house. She looked after me well.

Soon I had a couple of days off from the studio and went up to see Nan, also the play, at San Francisco. The sets and costumes were all very splendid, designed by Cecil Beaton. I had no doubt the play would succeed in New York, which indeed it did.

I have no recollections of anything exceptional happening during the shooting of *The Emperor Waltz* in the studio. The only unpleasantness I remember was as a result of two damn great white French poodles, which on several occasions appeared in scenes with Joan and me. I am very fond of dogs, I might even say devoted to them, indeed, there have been dogs that I have loved, but I don't want to act with the bloody animals, and I believe my aversion to doing so is shared with most actors. This particular pair of neatly clipped giant beasts were invariably held on a double leash by daughter, Joan, but she had no control over them. They would trip me up, get their leashes tangled with my sword, look up at me and yawn when I was in the middle of a long speech. I'm ashamed to admit that one long scene required twenty takes before we got it right. Truly, on perhaps six of these takes, I dried up, the hazards being too much for me. Well as I got on with Billy Wilder and little as I resented him lifting several hundred dollars from me in Jasper, I admit to feeling somewhat aggrieved when we finally got the shot in the can; he lost his cool and said:

'Cut, print at last! I thought you were a professional, Roland.'

I was ashamed, hot, frustrated, exhausted and hurt, all I could stutter was, 'Poo, Poo.'

I was unable to enunciate the second syllable to complete the word poodles!

We finished *Emperor Waltz* in August. I stayed through several weeks of September, in case of retakes, during which time Paramount offered me a two-picture a year deal, for two years. I talked this over with Tom Somlio and he settled a very satisfactory contract. This enabled me, if I wished, to play in a play and whilst in the play, such time would be added to the two years of my contract. Also, I might act in any other film by another company, providing it did not interfere with any plans that Paramount had for me, immediately. This also would extend the time of Paramount's use of my services. My contract was to start the first of December.

On the Sunday before leaving for New York, I had lunch at Charlie Brackett's. At this luncheon, there was a couple I had previously met at Charlie's, Dorothy Stickney and Howard Lindsay, her husband.

With my old friend Alan Wilkie and Kenny More at an hotel bathing pool in the south of France.

With Diana Dors and Donald Sinden feeding scotch to the star of *An Alligator Named Daisy*.

My ex-wife and I watching our sons
Michael and Robin play cricket and
(*far right*) Nan with Michael,
Lucinda and my grandson Roderic.

Michael's wedding.

Tina and family.

(*Left*) Rehearsing Menenius with Robert Hardy as Coriolanus.

(*Right*) Celia Johnson and myself outside the stage door of the O'Keefe Centre in Toronto during *Hay Fever*.

With John Gielgud in *Ivanov*.

Howard was an actor/playwright. He and Dorothy had recently been in a very successful play of his, which had run for two years on Broadway, *Life With Father*. Dorothy now had a play, not written by Howard, which was to go into rehearsal in December. It was not yet cast, and she asked me if I would be interested to play opposite her in this piece. She understood that I was going to New York the following week as they were themselves, so we could meet. I said I would be happy to read it. A script would be delivered to me at the Plaza Hotel where I was to stay for a couple of weeks before boarding the *Queen Elizabeth* for England.

As my financial future was assured for the next two years, with my Paramount contract, I had nothing to lose by doing a Broadway play, it would merely put back my contract for the length of the run of the play. Nan was waiting for me at the Plaza, having achieved adjoining rooms; obviously we were unable to stay there as man and wife. The script of the play had arrived before me. Nan had read it but was non-committal. I was not very impressed when I read it. It had some skill in writing and some amusing dialogue, but I could not see how in a light comedy such as it was Dorothy Stickney, a pretty, very feminine little woman, could be really sympathetic as an alcoholic, who had seen a genie, me, rise from a bottle. In the play, she had a young daughter, apparently unaware that her mother was a lush. In the end I appear as her doctor, but recognisable as the genie. I take her away to an inebriates' home. As I have described the bones of the story, it sounds impossible, nevertheless, it was skilfully constructed and in its way mine was a good part.

When I finished reading it I asked Nan's opinion. Nan is a very honest and downright character and a pretty good judge when she reads a play. Although she wanted me to rejoin her in New York as soon as maybe, when we discussed the play together she said she didn't think it was good enough. The two juvenile characters were nebulous and very sketchily drawn and the whole story improbable. However, she said that as it would cost me nothing if it was a flop, she saw no harm in accepting the job if I felt like it. But she said in ordinary circumstances I should say no.

Of course, I should have said no at once, but it was not that easy. Dorothy was in love with the play. How could I say to this New York star, whom I had only known for a short while, that I didn't think the play was very good. I met Dorothy and Howard. They talked me into it, that is, I agreed to play in it if my agents acquired a satisfactory contract with the management. I had telephoned Tom Somlio and asked him to arrange terms. He said not less than X dollars a week would do, particularly as I was not all that keen on the play. I left it at that.

That evening, I was to meet Dorothy and Howard and they were to take me to see Ethel Merman in *Annie Get Your Gun*, and we were all to sup after the show—Ethel Merman and Nan were to join us. It was a very pleasant evening, I thoroughly enjoyed the show and Ethel Merman's wonderful performance and we had an amusing supper party. But next day it was somewhat embarrassing, after having been entertained so generously the previous evening, to have to telephone Dorothy and say that my agents had not succeeded in coming to a satisfactory financial agreement with the management. The producers of this production were short of Tom Somlio's X dollars a week by several hundred. Negotiations continued through the week, and they upped their offer by a couple of hundred. But Tom stuck to his guns and the time came for my departure for England. Dorothy begged me to take the script with me in the hope that a compromise might be reached. Of course I agreed to do so but did not anticipate ever appearing in the play.

Now Nan and I had to part once more, for a while. She saw me off in the *Queen Elizabeth*. I was to return to join her again immediately after Christmas, which in spite of my divorce, due in November, I was to spend with my two sons. As usual, I thoroughly enjoyed my time in this beautiful ship but there is no room in this story for details of the voyage. While at sea, I had written off any thought of the play, when on the last day I received a cable from Tom saying, 'My terms agreed. You will have to do it. Rehearsals December 3. Tom.'

When I arrived in London, I now had about six weeks to tidy up my affairs before returning to New York for rehearsals. I lived in our Carlton Mews house. Daphne was granted her decree nisi in the middle of November, with the custody of our sons, but I had uninhibited access to them. I saw Daphne the same day and congenial arrangements were arrived at for all concerned. Now I had to face my mother with the news. It was an unhappy encounter and I do not propose to dwell on it. I attached no blame to anyone but myself and received the strict moral rebuke that I had anticipated. Mother, of course, finally forgave me, but Mother had been in the habit of forgiving me all my life.

Originally I simply headed this chapter *Home and Divorce*, but then I found that there were hardly more than a couple of paragraphs to write about those few weeks in London. I did not enjoy my temporary bachelorhood alone in Carlton Mews, unless winning and losing money at Crockford's on many evenings was pleasure. I saw most of my old friends and can recall no outstanding incidents, and come the end of November I boarded the *Queen Mary* for New York.

It so happened that Jack Minster, who had returned to England some several weeks previously, was again on his way to New York, also in the *Queen Mary*. I gave him the play to read, in which I was about to appear, and he thought it was a certainty.

'Cinderella story, dear boy,' he said, 'can't miss.'

I pointed out the improbability of a sympathetic Cinderella with DTs. He didn't think that mattered at all as the play was written.

This trip across the herring pond turned out to be rather different from my two previous crossings. We ran into a violent storm, which lasted nearly twenty-four hours. For a long time, we were reduced to five or six knots, green water breaking over the bows of the great ship. I am fortunately a good sailor, and sea-sickness is happily not one of my many weaknesses, but the main dining-room, on this occasion, was reduced to about fifty passengers. Jack Minster remained in his cabin, in a bad way, for over two days, as did hundreds of others.

However there was a lady on board who happened to be a good sailor. I had met her previously at the poker table at Crockford's and Bate's Clubs during the war. On the first night of the voyage, she suggested that we play gin rummy. Having learned the finer subtleties of the game the hard way with Billy Wilder I thought I could hold my own pretty well. At the end of the first evening I was winning, perhaps £40. We agreed to keep a washing list, and to settle up on the last day. I continued to win. I had a quite phenomenal run of good cards.

On the fourth evening I was winning, I recall, £245. The sea was much calmer now, but for some strange reason this rather surprisingly seemed to affect my lady opponent somewhat adversely. At about eleven o'clock she said, 'Oh dear, I feel really dreadful.' Then she rose shakily and said, 'I am so sorry. Please, Roland, help me to my state-room.'

We staggered out of the lounge and I left her at the door of her room. She was a rich lady, minks, sables, etc., and glittering with a large display of a 'girl's best friend'. But I never saw her again! She did not appear next day to either lunch or dinner and I did not collect my £245.

I have refrained from mentioning this lady's name for obvious reasons. But if she is still alive, and if by chance she should ever read this story and if perhaps its perusal makes her conscience at all uneasy, she can allay any pangs of remorse, quite simply, by sending me a cheque care of my publishers.

As a result of the storm we were eighteen hours late in New York. It had become probable on the last day that we would dock in the evening at a time when Nan would be at her theatre and unable to meet me.

When I left New York, Nan and I had been staying during my two weeks there at the Plaza, which is one of the most expensive hotels in New York, on the corner of Fifth Avenue and Fifty-Ninth Street, overlooking Central Park, so that when I left, it was clearly too expensive for me to leave her there during my stay in England. She moved into an apartment with a girlfriend in the play. I knew we would not be continuing together in this apartment, so I sent Nan this cable. I wished to make things quite clear.

> Owing to the storms this ship has been slowed down at times to five or six knots so I will be very late and may arrive at a time when you are in your theatre and unable to meet me at the dock. I have no idea where we are staying in New York. Please let me know by return cable lest you can't meet me. Love Roland.

Somehow I have never been able to abbreviate telegrams in a reasonable manner. Not the case with Nan who, with inborn Scottish thrift, did not regard verbose cables as money well spent. I received the following reply:

> Plaza. Nan.

The play I was about to rehearse was entitled *A Little For The Bottle*. It consisted of a cast of four characters, Dorothy, the mother alcoholic, myself, the genie-cum-doctor, the *ingénue* daughter and her boyfriend. We rehearsed for three weeks and as the days passed I became pretty sure that my first conclusions were correct. It was not going to work.

We opened in Boston, the notices cool, but not disastrous, but there were few laughs. We all worked very hard, rehearsing daily, trying to improve it, but to little effect. We then went to Philadelphia, where we were supposed to play for two weeks. However, the notices here were very rude and business worse. We only played a week and that was the end of that. We did not go to New York. Dorothy was sadly disappointed; she was as good as possible in the part, but the critics and public just would not accept the situation. So back I went to New york and my Paramount contract.

On my return to New York, Nan and I stayed in a hotel in Washington Square, where her girlfriend, Jeri Sauvinet, had her apartment. My dollar bank balance was not at the moment up to Plaza prices. *Lady Windermere* was still playing to excellent business and we all, that is Nan and I and the cast of *Windermere*, had a lot of fun in New York together.

I had only been back a few weeks when I was offered a part in a film, *Singapore*, a Universal picture, with Ava Gardner and Fred MacMurray. So once again my Paramount contract was delayed for another six weeks. I flew back to Tinsel Town, leaving Nan in New York in the play until her contract was up in a couple of weeks and she was able to join me.

I arrived at Universal Studios and was greeted by the producer and director, and introduced to Fred MacMurray and the lovely Ava Gardner, with whom I was to play most of my scenes. This ravishing brunette I had never met or indeed seen before, and my eyes must have sparkled with admiration.

Briefly, the film story was this, Ava had been in love with Fred MacMurray, then through an accident lost her memory and married me. Then Fred turns up again, she has another accident, the result of which, amnesia cured; Fred claims her and I lose her. There was a bit more to it than that, but who wants any more? I didn't want to lose her! I enjoyed making the film. Ava was nearly as much fun as she was beautiful, and Fred was also very good company.

Nan had duly arrived while I was in the middle of the film. We had promised ourselves a holiday at Del Monte Lodge, on Pebble Beach golf course—do I mean 'we', or do I mean 'I'?—as soon as the picture was over. We drove up to Del Monte where we had a charming suite on the first floor overlooking the eighteenth green and the ocean.

We had a happy two weeks on the beautiful Monteray peninsula and on returning to Los Angeles, accommodation by now being considerably easier to come by, we shared an apartment at the Château Marmont with Jimmy Woolf, Sir John Woolf the film producer's brother, who was learning a job at Universal Studios. At this time, Nan had become very friendly with Gladys Cooper's family; she had shared a dressing-room in the New York theatre in *Windermere* with Sally Cooper, Gladys's younger daughter. Now back in California, Sally returning soon after Nan, we continued to meet frequently.

While Nan and I and Jimmy were at the Château Marmont, we

went to numerous parties and gave a few ourselves. Names, names, names. It is possible that I am expected to drop several, but the hell of it is that I have forgotten lots of them. Anyway, they have all been dropped now so many times that they must be broken to pieces, poor things. A shattering thought. But I must mention that I met Greta Garbo at Gladys's house on a couple of occasions and was duly impressed. On the first occasion she was with actor Clifton Webb, an amusing chap. Indeed Garbo would be unlikely to be escorted anywhere by a bore. She, like Gladys, did not suffer fools gladly. My female readers may be interested to know her attire. I suppose because I was more than thrilled to meet her I happen to remember what she was wearing. She wore a dove-grey polo-necked cashmere pullover and grey linen slacks. I am afraid I am unable to go as far as her shoes! I could, of course, ask Nan, but I'm not going to.

At the end of May, I had an offer for a very good part in a London play which, sadly, it was not possible to accept. If I dodged between England and Hollywood, earning many dollars in the United States and considerably fewer pounds in England, it was pointed out to me that I would get into a most complicated income tax muddle. My accountant insisted that the only policy at the time was to become a resident alien while completing my Paramount contract. So the Inland Revenue compelled me to become an expatriate for the time being.

Nan was to leave me in California at the end of July, tidy up her affairs in England, and see her family and so on. Both our divorces were resolved and we were to be married in California on her return.

Before she left, we attended the première of *Emperor Waltz*, at the Paramount Theatre on Hollywood Boulevard—I think sometime in June, a very hot evening. At this time, before the Hollywood slump, the studio intended to build up my image as a rather superior English gent, a kind of younger C. Aubrey Smith. Although it was not in my contract to do so, the front office, so called—that is, the powers that be—expected their bald contract artistes on public occasions to either wear a toupee or a hat. By now I had played in four Hollywood pictures; in the first, *To Each His Own*, I had worn an iron-grey toupee; in *Down to Earth* I was resplendent in a snow-white toupee; in *Emperor Waltz* I was topped by a large brown, greying toupee, and in *Singapore* I donned a toupee matching my natural brown hair. This last was fashioned as near as maybe to my own hairstyle when young. So it seemed to me pretty fatuous to pretend to my public that all these different colours, shapes, fashions of hairdo's, grew naturally from my pate. However, on the occasion of the première of *Emperor Waltz*, I went along with the 'front office' and arrived with Nan, duly garbed in a dinner jacket and black trilby hat. Although it was a hot evening there was quite a strong breeze and toupees do not take kindly to wind. Hence the hat.

Now, on the occasion of a Bing picture, the crowds assembled on Hollywood Boulevard might well compare in numbers to those watching a coronation in the Mall, minus the Brigade of Guards. So it was on this very warm evening. Nan and I had an excellent early dinner and we were feeling no pain. As we alighted from our limousine, and mounted the several steps to the foyer, I was detained by a television reporter and requested to say a few words to the television camera.

He said, 'Mr Culver, would you please say a few words to our viewers? This is the very first time the celebrities of a Hollywood première have been televised.'

Naturally I accepted this invitation and stepped up before the camera. I said something to the effect that I hoped when everyone had seen the film they would enjoy it as much as I expected to do. Then I finished thus.

'I see this vast crowd lining the streets, watching the occasion, and you all look so comfortably dressed on this hot evening, in your T-shirts, shorts and linen slacks, whereas here am I in a very warm tuxedo, which indeed is quite right and proper on such an occasion. However, you may all wonder why on so very warm an evening, I should be wearing a hat. Perhaps you may think it is an idiosyncrasy peculiar to Englishmen. Not so, on these occasions should you see an actor wearing a hat, there is but one reason.'

Here I raised my hat high, revealing my bald pate, bowed, and said, 'Enjoy yourselves.'

Nan and I were in our seats, when a few minutes later Bing arrived in a hat! Poor chap, he didn't know what had hit him—an enormous burst of laughter and applause echoed down Hollywood Boulevard. When Bing was able to get a hearing he said, 'Well, thanks folks. I never realised I was accepted as such a funny man. Must say I can't see the resemblance but maybe you mistook me for Bob Hope.'

CHAPTER XIV

750 Napoli Drive

When Nan left for England, I also had to get out of the United States for a day and return with a resident alien visa. The nearest exit to the States was Mexico. I drove with a lady who arranged these things to San Diego, about a hundred miles from Los Angeles, stayed the night in an hotel after crossing to Tijuina, in Mexico, then drove back to Hollywood with my new visa.

The jitters in the Hollywood studios were shortly to begin. The tax England had put on American films to protect the British film industry, which the quota system had quite failed to do, was one problem. Another hazard was television competition which now looked positively disastrous. So very soon after I became a resident alien of the United States, it seemed unlikely that the studio would bother to spend time and money on building up my image; indeed, all the studios were becoming aware that they had a lot of expensive contract artists whom they would be unlikely to use as originally intended. But I had burned by boats, and now a resident alien, I was resigned not to be built up; nevertheless, determined to collect the money.

One Sunday, I drove Gladys Cooper back from a lunch party at Charlie Brackett's. Before her guests arrived for tea, Gladys showed me the smaller house she was having built on the adjoining land to her own. On our way back through the garden, Gladys said, 'I expect to move to the house in November and will rent 750 furnished. Would you like to take it on when you and Nan are married?'

750 Napoli Drive was always referred to as 750. At Gladys's suggestion, I didn't hesitate, and a rental was immediately agreed on. Of all the houses I might have picked up to live in, in Tinsel Town area, this would have been my first choice.

From the garden there was a magnificent view of the Riviera Golf

Course, and recently I had become a member of the club. Directly below the garden, perhaps fifty feet, was the fifth green; then looking away from the green over one's shoulder, to the left, was the length of the fifth fairway, bordered on the right (players' left) by tall eucalyptus trees. Looking across the fifth green, one saw the sixteenth green and part of the fairway and above that, about a height level with our garden, was the sixth green. Then again, but no, perhaps I should hesitate to become too eulogistic about the beauty of a golf course. For no doubt many non-golf fans may consider I am looking back through rose-coloured glasses. Suffice it, to me it was a divine view, and here I was to live, except for a short interval, for nearly two years.

I was forty-seven years of age. I considered it unlikely that in the future ever again would I be rich enough to live in such a perfect spot, with such golfing amenities. Very well, Paramount were not going to build me up, but they were to supply me with enough money to enable me to reduce my golfing handicap from eighteen to eleven and win a pot (cup) off that handicap by 1949. I cannot admit to shame or regret that I deserted my Thespian mistress for those two years for the thrill of hitting a little white ball some hundreds of yards, and then putting it into a little round hole in fewer and fewer strokes.

Several weeks before Nan returned from England, Gladys kindly invited me to be a house guest until Nan and I took over the house.

'Since you are here for tea every other day after your golf,' said Gladys, 'you'd better move in. It'll save you the trouble of driving twelve miles from the Château Marmont.'

I gratefully accepted this invitation. Jimmy Woolf had already decided to move to another flat, so I was not landing him with the rent of the double apartment.

In early August, Phyllis Calvert arrived in California to make a picture for Paramount. She was accompanied by her husband, a dear chap, Peter Murray Hill. They rented David Niven's house in Pacific Palisades. David was, I think, in England at the time of their arrival. I have not discovered whether it was one of David's practical jokes—I rather suspect that it was—but when Peter and Phyllis on the first morning of their stay crossed the lawn, perhaps a hundred yards or more from the house, to the swimming pool, where there were changing-rooms, ladies and gents adjoining, Peter stripped off in the gents and Phyllis in the ladies. Peter was surprised to see a plain glass partition separating the two changing-rooms, and there was his wife naked, apparently looking at him through the glass. But she was not looking at him, she was looking at herself. It was a one-way mirror.

Peter, unable to attract Phyl's attention, thought it a bit odd and walked round to her door, went in and discovered the cause. Peter explained the situation to Phyl, and said, 'I think perhaps we will have a curtain over that mirror. I really don't think it necessary to prove to all and sundry that you are a natural redhead!'

Jack Merivale, Gladys's stepson, who had recently arrived and was staying in the small house, Robert Coote, Philip Friend, married to Eileene Eiskine, Dickie Greene, and several others including myself, joined in many swimming parties at this pool, and as it sometimes abounded with lovely ladies, we were all rather resentful of Peter's shyness of the colour of his wife's pubic curls.

Nan arrived back on 30th September and we were married on 4th October, at the register office at Santa Monica. Willie, 'Nigel' Bruce, gave Nan away, Sally was bridesmaid, and Ian Hunter my best man. In case of publicity photographers, I went along with the 'front office' and wore a hat to the wedding. There was a group photograph taken, I standing on one step above Nan, who in high heels is apt to top me by half an inch. This photograph was seen in England by my good friend Hygh Williams, known as Tam, who is reported to have unkindly remarked, 'Look at silly little Roly in a hat, pretending to be a six-footer.'

Almost immediately after our marriage, Gladys and Sally left for England, leaving us alone in 750. Not quite alone, as we took on Gladys's coloured cook-cum-housemaid, a charming, very shy girl named Jewel. She was indeed very properly named; treasure is the Victorian appellation for such a servant.

The year 1947 passed happily in this house, I playing golf most days, usually with Willie Bruce and an American actor Willard Parker; sometimes Rex would join us, also Bob Coote. One memorable incident stays with me when playing with Rex. The four-ball on this occasion was Jack Merivale, Willie B, Rex and myself. We were standing on the seventh tee, where one had to drive over perhaps fifty yards of rough. Running along the right-hand side of the fairway was a veritable jungle where, if a ball was sliced badly, there was practically no chance of finding it again. As one of us prepared to drive off, a ball retriever—that is a chap that searched the course for lost balls, and sold them to some players, a practice not encouraged by the club but quite impossible to control—offered a box of a dozen balls to Rex for $5. However, Rex said, 'Go away fellow, go away. I don't buy balls from you chaps. Hop it.'

The chap hopped it some yards away from the tee and watched us drive. I was all right, my ball landed on the fairway, as did Willie Bruce's. Come Rex, he hit an almighty slice, the ball vanishing into the distant undergrowth on the right. A second ball followed, and a third. Rex was tenacious, and two more balls made similar graceful elliptic curves into the wilds. By this time he found that he had no more balls in his bag. He looked across at the ball retriever and beckoned him over. 'Give me that box of balls,' said Rex. 'Five dollars. Here you are.'

Said the retriever, 'Sorry, buddy, the market has gone up. Seven bucks.'

'Hell,' said Rex. 'Seven dollars for a box of old balls. Rubbish.'

Said the retriever, 'All pretty new, pal. Look at 'em.'

By this time Willie, Jack and I were beginning to get the giggles.

Rex said, 'Oh, give me the damn things. There's your money.'

So the deal was made. Rex teed up one of the balls, gave it a mighty swipe and it landed on the fairway, thirty or forty yards ahead of Willie's and mine. Said Rex, with a grin, 'I think I've got this game licked.' We all laughed, and as far as I remember, Rex did not lose another ball that day.

The months passed and still my services were not required at the studio until April 1948, when I was asked if I could play the part of a Southern Colonel. I had no desire to play a Southern Colonel, but, had I said I couldn't play it, my agent advised me that that would end my contract as I had no script approval. So I agreed, but said I assumed that they would supply me with someone to coach me with the accent. They assured me they would do so. I took the script home and of its kind it wasn't a bad part, but I thought a fairly poor story.

I was called to the studio a day or two later to meet my speech coach, who turned out to be an attractive young woman, in her early thirties, with an elegant figure and beautiful legs. But as far as I was concerned, there was one drawback to this handsome creature, she stood six foot seven in her stockinged feet—roughly six feet eight and a half in moderately high heels. In other words, a foot taller than myself.

Once we started shooting, she never left my side. Naturally, I was the butt of the Paramount lot. Bing and Bob Hope had a ball with their wisecracks. 'Roly, if you like it standing up, borrow a ladder from props.' Or, 'Go to the Riviera stables, I guess they will lend you a mounting block.' Bing and Bob were not my only tormentors, even Charlie Brackett threw out the odd *bon mot*. But I survived all this ribaldry, and the girl seemed to think it great fun and took no offence.

In the film, Veronica Lake played one of my daughters, not a very good part, but a contract artiste the studio had lost interest in. She was a charming girl and keen actress. In 1959 when I was in New York with *Five Finger Exercise*, she visited me in my dressing-room, thoroughly disillusioned with Tinsel Town and happy to be in New York. A nice person.

The picture completed I returned with improving skill to the golf course and won the pot I mentioned earlier.

Judith Fellows, an actress friend of Nan's, had replaced Penelope Dudley-Ward as Lady Windermere for the tour of the play, finished in San Francisco and came to stay with us for a couple of weeks. Whilst with us she had the extraordinary experience of attending an Atwater Kent party. Atwater Kent was a strange little millionaire who gave enormous parties. I used to wonder how many people were gate-crashers. The food was never very good at these affairs but there was plenty of booze. One saw very little of one's host; in fact on one occasion I didn't see him at all.

It was when Judy was staying with us that Rex's tragedy with poor Carole Landis occurred.

One day, when as usual I had been playing golf, I returned home at perhaps 4.30 to find the house empty. I assumed that Nan and Judy were next door, either in or by the pool with Gladys, who had returned from England. So I strolled through to the pool to find Gladys, but no Nan or Judy. I asked where they were. Gladys told me the news that was to splash over the headlines. Carole Landis, who was in love with Rex, had taken an overdose of sleeping-pills. After a cry for help from Rex over the telephone Nan and Judy had gone straight round to Carole's house and they had been there some three hours or more.

When Nan and Judy finally returned to 750, Nan explained the details which are now well known, that Carole had at sometime the previous night taken this overdose and was dead when Rex arrived at her house at lunchtime.

The next day the balloon went up. Tittle, tattle, typewriters rattle, the press went into battle. Hedda Hopper, Louella Parsons, Sam Sewerpen, Gay Gossip, Syd Smearem and Uncle Tom Cobley and all had Rex with his back to the wall. But a miracle had happened. Along the front garden of 750 there ran a brick wall, about seven feet high, at the centre of which was a tall gate, and a path leading from the gate to the front door of the house. But this gate, and this front door, was seldom, if ever, used. It was our custom, and that of our guests, to enter the house by the side entrance, where there was a large drive leading to the garage with plenty of other parking space.

After my golf on the day of the tragedy, I had invited Willard Parker and the assistant golf pro to come and have a drink with us at six o'clock. They duly arrived but for some reason parked outside our front gate. There they discovered two small cases, and a note fixed to one of them to Rex. The note and the cases were from Carole. She had clearly dumped them there in the middle of the night before her death, where they had remained all day without being discovered. Had the press thought of querying Rex's statement that he had been with me the previous evening, as he had been, and paid me a visit, they would doubtless have entered the house at the front door and been the first to discover the note and the cases, which Rex explained to me contained all their most intimate possessions, letters, photographs and presents that Rex had given Carole. It was bad luck on the columnists. They missed that scoop.

Lilli, who had been away from California, hoping, I think, that the affair would burn itself out, flew back as soon as she heard the news, to stand loyally by Rex's side through his ordeal. Nan and I went to the funeral with them at Forest Lawn. A grotesque occasion, the misery of which I will leave to the imagination of my readers. Judy left us the day before the funeral and Gladys's parting remark was, 'Well, Judy, you can tell them at home that we have done you proud. You have really seen Hollywood. You have been to an Atwater Kent party and been involved in a suicide.'

About a week after this, Rex and Lilli thought it desirable to get, right away from the atmosphere of Tinsel Town, and Nan and I went with them for a few days respite to Del Monte Lodge. While Rex and I played golf at Pebble Beach and Cyprus Point, Nan and Lilli explored the Monteray peninsula. We had travelled in separate cars so we were independent. I think the change did them both good. I hoped so.

In June, Gladys said she was very sorry, but she wanted us to leave 750 for a couple of months as her daughter Joan and husband Robert Morley, and their two children Sheridan and Annabelle, were coming out for a holiday before Robert started rehearsals for the New York production of his play, *Edward, My Son*, in September, and she would like the house for them. We now rented a friend's house on the cliff side, overlooking Santa Monica. We had invited Nan's mother to visit us for the summer, and she arrived a day or two after we moved to this house. By the time she arrived, we had discovered a most unpleasant drawback to this place. I was awakened in the night with the sensation of something crawling on my bottom. I turned over quickly and felt some creature squash. I jumped out of bed to find the remains of a dead cockroach in the sheets. Early next day, we found the house to be literally swarming with the horrid insects. Whether the friends from whom we had rented this house were indifferent to the presence of these beasties, or kept them as pets, or whether it was a new and sudden invasion, we never learnt; but we didn't like it, and when Marjorie, Nan's mother, arrived, she didn't like it either.

We had only been there a few days when Gregory Peck asked me if I would care to play the leading part in *Rope*, in a small theatre he and Mel Ferrer ran in La Jolla. There would be little money in it, but enough to pay my hotel bill and he thought I might enjoy a short theatrical exercise. I knew the play well and the part is very effective and I thought I might find it fun and worth sacrificing my golf for a couple of weeks or more.

The play *Rope* was founded on fact. Two undergraduates merely for a bet murdered some perfectly harmless youth, put his corpse in an oak chest and gave a party in the room where this chest was part of the furniture. The actual case was a *cause célèbre*. In the play my character is a slightly eccentric guest at the party and through the action he gradually deduces what has happened. The last act is very tense when he discloses the horror of the evening. The play was written by Patrick Hamilton. I haven't read it since but I have an idea that it would stand a revival. I don't remember who directed the production at La Jolla, but it was well done.

This engagement at La Jolla was all settled very quickly. Nan and I discussed it, of course, and I said, 'I'm sorry, darling, to leave you, but I do think I should get a little theatre practice.' Nan was really very reasonable about it and off I went to La Jolla, about seventy miles south. I think we were to have ten days' rehearsals for the play and a week playing. I settled myself comfortably into a very pleasant room in a charming hotel. We had a long day's rehearsal next day, and I arrived back at the hotel bang on time for a sundowner, so made my way straight to the lounge bar, where I immediately saw Nan and Marjorie. Nan, happily sipping a large whisky and water, and Marjorie, I think, a gin and tonic. 'Oh, oh, oh! hello darling,' I said.

Nan said, 'Hello, darling. We felt you might be lonely, so we thought we would come and stay with you.'

Said I, 'Good heavens, who's going to look after the beetles!'

That theatre engagement for Gregory Peck was not for me a financial success.

After La Jolla, we went back to the house at Santa Monica, but we only stayed there a few more days. It was too unpleasant. And I decided to cut my losses and find other accommodation. It so happened that Rex, once again, came into the picture. He was in trouble now of a different nature, indeed, the sort of trouble he had warned me in Paris that I might get into. Tax trouble.

Being aware of my own irresponsibility when earning big money, I had passed the buck to my accountant who made me a strict allowance. Rex, however, had somehow been ill-advised and was in a financial jam. He was about to go with Lilli to New York, to prepare for *Anne of a Thousand Days*, and wanted to leave his young son, Carey, with his nanny in the house. Although it was a large house, who would rent it while occupied by a child and a nanny? I was the answer. There was plenty of room for Carey, and nanny, and Nan, and Marjorie and myself. So I rented the house on the understanding that we would move back to 750 Napoli in September, when the Morley family had moved out.

This we did. Marjorie returned home to England and time continued to pass in a very pleasant manner, until about Christmas, when I awakened one morning and looked out of the window at an impossibility. The Riviera Golf Course was hidden under a blanket of three or four inches of snow. A couple of blue birds and a robin naturally—well to European eyes, not quite naturally, as North American robins are about the size of a mistle thrush—were hopping about our garden, obviously wishing that they could change into penguins. They were very puzzled birds, and it was a very puzzled and outraged Tinsel Town. Snow! What did God think he was up to? Certainly a joke in very poor taste. That snow remained, covering the ground, for twenty-four hours.

I was finally called back to the studio in April, near the end of my contract, to play in a picture, *The Great Lover*, with Bob Hope. It was by no means one of Bob's best pictures, but it was of course great fun to do. Bob's job in life is to make people laugh and many wisecracks during the production came daily. No extra money for making the cast and technicians laugh—he did that for free.

Also in the cast was my friend Roland Young, with whom I had played in a film in England during the war. The Bob Hope picture was finished early in May, and my contract over.

That ended my days in Tinsel Town. The years spent there did little to enhance my reputation as an actor, but for much of the time I had lived in a charming house, had dear friends and was able to indulge in several sports that I enjoyed; swimming, riding and golf. I do not regret my stay, neither did I regret leaving sunny California, to return to my proper milieu.

When Nan and I left for home, we spent ten days in New York, where we had a feast of theatres. We saw *Kiss Me Kate*, a matinée of *Where's Charlie* with Ray Bolger, a delightful afternoon, the same evening, *South Pacific*, with the original cast, Mary Martin, Enzio Pinza. We saw Rex in *Anne of a Thousand Days*, Robert in *Edward, My Son*. Altogether, I began to feel very homesick for the theatre, and a longing to get back to it. Fortunately, I didn't have to wait long.

Soon after arriving home, Bill Linnet sent me a play to read, by a comparatively new author, one William Douglas Home. The play, entitled *Master of Arts*, I thought a lot of fun. I accepted the job, and we opened at Southsea, on try-out, but there was no London theatre available, and Bill Linnet thought it best to lay off until the autumn.

Quite naturally, when I first returned to England, I saw my mother and father, who had returned to London. My sons, now at prep school near Crawley, I visited with Daphne, who had not yet married again, but later married a very nice doctor, and still later decided on another change.

When the production of *Master of Arts* was postponed, Nan and I, with Sally Cooper and Jack Merivale, now in England, went for a holiday—as if I hadn't had a paid holiday for the last two years—to Monte Carlo, where we were joined for part of the time by Rex and Lilli, Rex's play having closed in New York some weeks previously. Also my old friend Jack Minster turned up. Once again the casino used its magnetism on me many evenings. We all had a very pleasant time, in the Mediterranean sun, although I'm afraid Nan, quite justifiably, became somewhat bored with the casino. After this holiday, we re-rehearsed *Master of Arts* and opened at the Strand Theatre in September. Playing opposite me was the charming actress, Ursula Howells. The play was not a smash hit, but we ran about five months and I enjoyed it.

It was William Douglas Home's fourth play. I played the character of a house-master at a public school, obviously Eton but not identified as such in the programme. My character gets into all kinds of scrapes as a result of the machinations of a schoolboy whom I am discovered caning at the opening of the play. It was a very light comedy, and I finish up with Ursula Howells in my arms. No objection to that.

In January, I received horrifying information from my accountant. It seemed that I was in the income tax cart, which I had thought to have avoided. The Inland Revenue claimed that I owed them the difference between United States and British tax for three years. I have always been brought up to believe it vulgar to mention one's bank account or large earnings, though this reticence does not of course apply to film stars or boxing champions, and, I regret to say, golfers. But as I only consider myself a supporting film actor, though a stage and television star, I do not feel myself privileged, if that is the right word, to mention the sum the Revenue were expecting me to pay. Suffice it, that it was an amount I did not possess.

My accountants had a long battle over this assessment, claiming, quite correctly, that I had been a resident alien of the United States for over two years. The Revenue maintained that I had premises in London. This however was not so. The house in Carlton Mews was leased by my wife eighteen months before we were married, and all the contents hers. I had no possessions in England, as my ex-wife now owned everything else I had had. This battle with the Revenue lasted several months, when finally my accountants won a partial victory. The Revenue conceded the point of two years' residency in the United States, but insisted that I must pay for my first year there. That included my work in *Down to Earth* and *Emperor Waltz*—my largest earnings in Hollywood; the amount they claimed was still, I think, at least four times more than my then bank balance. What to do? I could have gone bankrupt, but I shrank from that idea in horror. A friend of mine had had that uncomfortable experience during the war, and I wanted none of it.

My accountants now made a deal with the Revenue. I would pay them X-thousand pounds down and fifty per cent of all my future earnings as I received them, until the debt was paid off. At first the Revenue wanted fifty per cent of my gross earnings, that is before the ten per cent to my agent. This would have meant that I was only left with forty per cent and still be liable for tax on one hundred per cent of my current earnings. They finally agreed to fifty per cent of my net earnings. At the time, I saw no possibility of ever getting out of the red. It took me seven years to do so.

In August 1950, Binkie sent me a new Terence Rattigan play entitled *Who is Sylvia?* It was not one of Terry's greatest plays, but it was fun, and I enjoyed it. We opened at the Criterion Theatre in October, and ran eleven months. Bobby Flemyng and I played two friends who, in the first act, started at an age of around thirty and thirty-five respectively. In the second act we were in our fifties, and in the last act in our late seventies.

I had the rather easier process of getting older than Bobby. I wore an illustrious toupee in the first act, in the second act a somewhat receding one with a bald patch on the crown, then no toupee in the last act, just my bald head. Bobby, several years younger than myself, with plenty of brown hair, was compelled to grey his hair for the second act, and plaster white greasepaint on for the last act.

During the run of *Sylvia*, Bobby proposed me for membership of the Garrick Club, and many pleasant days and evenings have I spent there since. Sometime after the play came off, I played the same part in the film, then entitled *The Man Who Loved Red-Heads*. John Justin played Bobby's part, Moira Shearer played Diane Hart's part, and Gladys Cooper the wife. Alexander Korda produced *Redheads*, and Harold French directed it.

Between 1950 and 1960, I was fortunate enough to make many more films, among them two Somerset Maugham stories, *Sanatorium* and *The Ant and the Grasshopper*, one with Jean Simmons when still in her teens, and one with Nigel Patrick. Both of which I enjoyed. I made *Hotel Sahara*, *Folly to be Wise*, *Safari* and a number of other pictures, the titles of which I have forgotten. Several of these films I worked in while playing in the theatre at night, *Folly to be Wise* I made while playing in *The Deep Blue Sea*. Another film, among the forgotten titles, I also made during the run of that play. This one was mostly made on a location a few miles from Thame. I had a chauffeur to pick me up at the theatre each evening, when about five miles from my destination I would swallow a sleeping-pill to make sure of going straight to sleep when in between the sheets, perhaps sometime after midnight, since I would have to be up in the morning at 7 to go to work. Needless to say, I was pretty exhausted at times, and was paying dearly for my two years of comparative idleness in California. Nevertheless, I must have been very fit, as I managed to get a certain amount of golf in at weekends. And this continual work finally enabled me to get square with the tax man.

It had been a struggle. I had my two sons' education to pay, first their prep school and then their public school. So I admit to giving myself a slight pat on the back in 1957, when I received from my agent my first week's pay cheque of one hundred per cent net of my earnings.

CHAPTER XV

Tragedy and Comedy

While I had been in the United States, my sister Evelyn had become progressively more deranged. She had no moment of happiness, and was becoming unmanageable. The doctors at Northampton persuaded my parents to allow them to perform a frontal leucotomy. That is an operation on the frontal lobes of the brain. It is not desirable, neither am I able, to give a technical explanation of this operation; but a brief one is that it should separate the imagination from reality. The surgeons explained the operation was extremely delicate and did not guarantee complete success, but maintained that it would if even partially successful relieve her constant torment. Her illness, of course, had been a source of continual worry and unhappiness to my parents for twenty years. The operation was performed in 1950 and was successful, in so far as it quietened her down, but it brought no immediate return to normality. Unhappily, my mother did not live long enough to see her daughter out of hospital and able to read, write, laugh and work grospoint as she was by 1953. She then went to live in Tunbridge Wells with a charming friend of my mother's, and spent some of her time with Nan and me in the country. But she did not have many years of life left on her return to sanity. She died, happily, in her sleep in 1960, while I was in the United States once again, this time in *Five Finger Exercise*. I received quite a sensible and intelligent letter from her in New York a few weeks before she died.

My younger sister, Iris, had also been ill, but she did not write and concern me about herself, and I knew nothing of her illness until I returned home from *Five Finger Exercise*. Unhappily, she also died a few months after my return. This loss was a great sadness for me, as all our lives we had been very close.

It was during the run of *The Deep Blue Sea* that my adored mother died. I had visited her one Saturday morning before my matinée. Early Sunday morning Iris telephoned me and told me Mother had suffered a stroke that day.

When I saw Mother lying there, I knew she would never speak to me again. Yet the doctors kept her breathing for two weeks, with feeding tubes and such-like. I, of course, had to continue playing each day in Terry's sad play. Every night I would sleep in my parents' house, hoping for a miracle, yet knowing it could not be. She never regained consciousness. Father, ill himself at the time, never recovered from the shock, but lingered on miserably for three years. How splendid it would have been if the poor old chap had died the same day as Mother. But God is not that merciful.

My memory still insists in associating Mother's death with *The Deep Blue Sea,* and somehow, those other sadnesses too are crowded together in my mind. Perhaps because *The Deep Blue Sea* was a very sad play and the play I now want to write about. Yet another Terry Rattigan success.

Binkie sent me the script to read about Christmas time, 1951, telling me that Peggy Ashcroft had agreed to play Hester Collyer, so that I was able to read it visualising Peggy in the part. I was riveted, and did not put the play down—even to light a cigarette. I was somewhat surprised that I should have been asked to play William Collyer, as it was not the sort of character I was usually offered.

Perhaps I should explain that since the start of my career except for John Gabriel Borkman in rep, the tour of *Sun Up*, the part with Larry in *A Stranger Within*, the cockney corporal in *Suspense* and the villain in *Distinguished Gathering*, I had always been cast in light comedy roles and Sir William Collyer was very far from light comedy; indeed one might say tragedy. So I was mad keen to play it.

I went to see Binkie, and told him what a splendid play I thought it, and with Peggy I felt sure that it couldn't miss.

'Who,' I asked, 'is cast for Freddie Page?' A wonderful part and very important.

'It is not quite settled. We are thinking of——' and Binkie mentioned a certain actor's name.

I knew this actor well, also his work. He was a very talented chap, but I considered utterly miscast for the character of Freddie Page.

'Oh no,' I said to Binkie. 'A bloody good actor, but, oh no, not for Freddie Page. I'll tell you the fellow you want. I hardly know him, but I saw him in a play with Ronnie Squire, a Lonsdale play, can't remember the name. This part, I promise you, is tailor-made for him.'

I was very insistent, and Binkie promised that he would persuade Frith Banbury, who was to direct the play, to let Kenny Moore read it. They would arrange an audition the following week.

Quite by chance, the next day being fine, I decided to play golf at Wimbledon Park Golf Club, and whom should I find there but Ronnie Squire and Kenny playing together. When I saw them in the clubhouse, I said to Kenny, 'This is a hell of a coincidence.' I then told him about the play and my conversation with Binkie, the previous day.

Kenny thanked me and said, 'Is it really such a wonderful part?'

'My dear boy,' I said, 'the part of a lifetime, and a bloody sight better than mine.'

And a part of a lifetime it proved to be. Kenny read for it, as did the other actor, but there was never really any doubt who would play the part.

We rehearsed for about a month and went for a try-out to Cardiff. The weather being fine, Kenny and I played golf most days, and Peggy would sometimes walk round with us.

When we came to London in March, we were an immediate smash hit. The play and cast had splendid press. Peggy had wonderful notices, as did Kenny; in spite of the formidable competition, as far as I remember, I very nearly held my own with the critics. Although it was a very sad play, except for my sadness at Mother's death, we were a happy and jolly company. Peggy had been contracted to play for some months, and then given a holiday for six weeks, and Celia Johnson took over the part for that time. Naturally, she also gave a brilliant performance. Then Peggy returned for a time and once again left us, and Googie Withers took over, also giving a moving interpretation of Hester Collyer.

Comparisons are odious, suffice it to misquote and say, 'How happy I could play with either, where other dear artistes away.'

At the beginning of June 1953, I had agreed with Binkie to play in *The Little Hut* in New York in the autumn. Meanwhile, Freddie Lonsdale had asked Binkie to persuade me to direct a revival of one of his plays, *Aren't We All?* to open at the Haymarket Theatre in August. Nan and I with my sister Iris and her husband, first had a holiday at St Jean Cap Ferrat.

After our holiday, which provided many laughs—always the case when Iris was around—I immediately started work on the play, and we went into rehearsal in July. The cast included Ronnie Squire,

Marie Lohr, Jane Baxter, George Howe and Marjorie Fielding, all accomplished light-comedy performers. But my two young juvenile men had had little or no experience in this sort of comedy. I spent much time working with them on one particular scene, but I quite failed to get it anywhere near right. Up to a point I enjoyed my first job as director, but found it frustrating and unrewarding spending a lot of time trying to teach my two juvenile men how to play comedy. It was an impossible task. I remember Ronnie Squire complaining of the time I spent at rehearsals on this scene with these chaps. 'Come on, Roly,' he said, 'the rest of us want some direction and rehearsing. You can't turn a donkey into a racehorse.' Cecil Beaton designed the sets and costumes and it was a charming and expensive production.

On the opening night I stood at the back of the dress circle with butterflies fluttering about in my tummy, to watch my first-ever London direction, hoping my two young men would get a few laughs, but doubting it. But my first shock was nothing to do with the two boys; come Ronnie Squire's cue for entrance, he failed to appear. What for the love of Pete had happened? I took off and rushed down from the circle, reached the pass door, and still no Ronnie. The fellow must have dropped down dead, I thought.

As I appeared through the door on to the stage, Ronnie, who had been happily chatting to Marie in the wings, came to life. 'My God,' he said. 'I'm off.' And on he dashed. But there had been a stage wait of perhaps a minute or more. I went miserably back to my stand in the circle. Ronnie, with his charm and humour, soon got the audience on his side, but that missed entrance, somehow, caused the loss of tempo to the production. It never had the snap in it that it had at the dress rehearsal. The boys, I fear, got no laughs at all in what should have been a very amusing scene. A disappointing evening.

The production got a mixed press, but better than I expected. I was, I remember, criticised for the slowness of my direction. But I refused to take the blame for it. The play lasted twelve minutes longer than at the dress rehearsal, and those twelve minutes were not accounted for by laughter. Ronnie, as always, got his fair share, as did Marie and Marjorie. Jane got the few that were expected of her, as did George Howe. I called a rehearsal next day and jollied up the cast, and the second night the play lasted six or seven minutes less. After that, I had to leave them to their own devices as I was starting rehearsals for *The Little Hut*.

I hope I haven't given the impression that I blame Ronnie entirely for the loss of pace on that first night; everyone slowed down. Ronnie has been dead these several years, but we were great friends to the end, and that evening he could not have been more apologetic for his missed entrance.

I had some doubts about accepting the job to play in *The Little Hut* in New York. Before Robert Morley had the script Binkie had asked Rex Harrison and me to play in it. For some reason Rex and I could not do it at that time. When I first read the script the set was described as a sandy desert island with one palm tree and a couple of huts. But when I first saw the play in London, the set—by Oliver Messel—was a very lush jungle affair with all sorts of pantomime props. Robert making his first entrance carrying a butterfly net and two enormous butterflies the size of crows. None of these things made me laugh when I saw the production and I noticed I was not alone with my po-face. I believe I am right in saying that Robert was not too happy either with the set or the props. However, as we know, the play was a big success in London, so why not New York? I accepted the job.

Peter Brook directed *The Little Hut*, as in London. I played Robert Morley's part, and Anne Vernon the French actress played my wife, and Colin Gordon, David Tomlinson's part. Peter directed it at a cracking pace, as in London, with the same set and props. We opened in England for a try-out in Brighton, and it went like a bomb. However, my good friend Bob Coote, who had had a lot of experience in New York, saw me afterwards and said:

'All very well at Brighton, old boy, but if you play it at that pace in New York, they won't understand a bloody word. What with your English accent and Colin's, which is the sort of English accent Americans imitate as a joke, and Anne Vernon's ever-so-French accent, you've got a proper mix-up. You must tell Peter to slow it down. As for all those pantomime props, giant butterflies, three gramophones and windmill razors, they will never get it, old man. Never get it. Tell Peter Brook to simplify the whole thing, or you'll go for a proper burton.'

I said I would mention the pace problem to Peter, but I was not hopeful that he would listen to Bob's advice. As for the props, I said that I thought they were Peter's own invention and they amused him.

'Well,' said Bob, 'You take my tip, mate, or you will be playing golf with me in England before Christmas.'

Bob might well have written our New York notices, so accurate was he with his prediction. The New York critics also said that the play was immoral and distasteful. As to that, the New York theatre would seem to have altered its taste and morality since 1953. But I was back playing golf with Bobby, before Christmas! After reading the New

York notices I sent this cable to Robert: 'All Messeled up and drowned in the brook.'

On returning from New York in November, having had my game of golf with Bob, I was engaged to play in a film, *Hotel Sahara*, with Yvonne de Carlo, Peter Ustinov and David Tomlinson. The whole picture was very cleverly shot in the studios. On 1st January, a very cold day, I had to have a swimming scene with Yvonne, in a pool which represented an oasis in the desert. Naturally, it was heated and I was in and out of this pool all day. The publicity department had invited the press down to watch this scene, and perhaps get some glamorous pictures of Yvonne bathing. I, as usual, at that time, was wearing an excellent toupee, but for this scene I had an extra one as toupees do not take kindly to being plunged in and out of water. I had thought the make-up department had securely stuck on this hairpiece, to resist the many dives I might have to take into the pool. But after two or three hours, I rose from a dive and the damn thing floated off! I grabbed it and held it aloft saying, 'Cut, I've been scalped!'

There was considerable laughter and I retired to make up, and the hair was dried and firmly stuck on again. The following day, covering the whole of the front page of the *Daily Mirror*, was a picture of me taken from the back, showing my bald pate and holding my toupee up with this caption underneath: 'Roland Culver, bathing with Yvonne de Carlos, loses his toupee. Was his face red!'

No doubt the chap that took that photograph considered that he had been pretty smart, and the fellow who wrote the caption, a great wit. My face was far from red. It was blue with cold, but grinning.

Hotel Sahara was completed in early March. In August I started rehearsing for *Simon and Laura* opposite Coral Browne. The cast also included two talented young Thespians, Ian Carmichael and Dora Bryan and of course Ernest Thesiger. Coral is always grand company and we all had a lot of fun with the play. We toured for a number of weeks before coming to the Strand Theatre in November. Ian and Dora gave splendid performances and there was a happy team spirit in the company, but I have to confess that there was one scene in the play where we were all prone to the giggles, however not uncontroll-able and the audiences were usually with us. We were a fair success and ran several months.

In the early spring of 1955, while Gladys was playing in New York, Nan and I once again went to live in her home. This time Barn Elms at Henley. It was a beautiful spring and there was a lovely view from our bedroom window showing the lawn in the foreground then the river and meadows beyond, and the Chiltern Hills in the background.

Day after day, there would be a clear blue sky, with the sun brightly lighting up this landscape. Being idle at the time, I suddenly had an urge to paint this peaceful picture. So I bought myself some oil paints, read a book on painting and sat up in that bedroom each morning early, and tried to capture that gentle beauty. As it was the first oil painting I had ever attempted, the result was not unpleasing. I tried several other subjects, but they were not, I considered, worth keeping, except for a self-portrait in an oil sepia wash which Nan liked, and it hangs in our bedroom. The river painting hangs in our sitting-room. Then I attempted a few more canvases, but I decided that I would never become an RA.

In July of 1955, I accepted a part in a film, *Safari*, to be shot at first in the MGM Studios at Elstree, and afterwards we were to go on five or six weeks' location in the wilds of Kenya, living under canvas. Janet Leigh was the leading lady, I was her fiancée—or was it husband?—and Victor Mature, the fellow who won her in the end, but over my dead body! I was killed by the Mau-Maus. No tears to be shed by the audience at my demise; I was not a very pleasant character.

We had completed three weeks of shooting in the studios for *Safari*, with three days to go before flying to Nairobi. On the Sunday afternoon, I was playing tennis in the garden of Barn Elms, a doubles game, with Nan and her sister and brother-in-law. I was pretty hot and tired in the first game of the third set, when running to retrieve a ball, Paris shot me in the ankle. My Achilles tendon burst with a resounding crack. I went down in agony. I was silent for a moment, unable to utter, such was the pain. Recovering my voice, my language vied almost successfully with what my father's, or Lucille La Vern's, might have been in similar circumstances.

Nan asked me what was wrong and I said that I had bust my bloody Achilles tendon. Nan, rather surprisingly I thought, unfeelingly said that I was talking nonsense and that I couldn't have done; she once had a boyfriend who whilst chasing her in the garden jumped over a hedge and tore his Achilles tendon and rolled on the ground crying his eyes out. This reception of my statement did not exactly sooth my temper or moderate my language. I replied something to the effect that I didn't give a damn what her piddling, grizzling boyfriend did and I didn't get any relief from crying my eyes out. I knew, I said, that I had broken my bleeding tendon and that it was fucking agony and suggested that if she was so unhelpful she could buzz off and leave me to swear in peace.

I do not as a rule talk to Nan in this fashion, and she was now convinced that I had indeed busted my tendon, and became most concerned and solicitous. 'My darling,' she said, 'we must get a doctor at once.'

Peter, my brother-in-law, helped Nan carry me to the sitting-room. I could not put my foot to the ground. I lay on the sofa with my leg up, and a very large scotch in my hand, while Nan telephoned. But it was Sunday evening, we had as yet not required a doctor in Henley, and Nan was unable to contact one. Finally, it was decided to drive me to the casualty ward at a hospital in Reading, where we saw a very junior doctor on duty, I think a student. He confirmed the busted tendon, but could do little for me. He strapped it up, injected a pain killer, which I certainly needed, and advised me to contact a specialist in the morning. Fortunately I had a late call at the studio next day. Even so, quite clearly, I could not work on one leg and a crutch. I decided to pass the buck to the studio next morning. They would get the best advice.

First thing the following day I telephoned the studio, the producer was extremely concerned. 'Will you be able to work today?' he asked.

'I think it most unlikely, as I can only stand on one leg!' I said.

'Can you get to the studio soon?'

'Yes,' I said, 'my wife will drive me.'

'Well, come as quickly as you can and we will have the best man for the job. Leave it to me.'

My part in this picture was a large and important one, and I had appeared in perhaps two dozen scenes in the studio over the previous three weeks. If I was unable to continue, and the part recast, all that work would have to be reshot, and cost the production a bomb, all the schedules switched round and after Kenya, three extra weeks in the studio. Of course, insurance companies were involved in this situation. It so happened that I had an accident insurance policy of my own at that time which guaranteed me £100 a week if incapacitated. Not exactly the money I was earning in the film, but some comfort.

The studio altered the schedule for Monday's shooting and a studio car drove me to London to a surgeon, a Mr Tucker, who confirmed my worst fears. My tendon was completely severed, and he wanted to operate immediately. That news put the cat among the pigeons with a vengeance. 'Could nothing be done,' the studio asked, 'to postpone the operation until completion of the film and our visit to Kenya?'

After consultation with the insurance companies it was agreed that if I finished the film and then had my operation it would not deprive me of my own insurance for the time I would be unable to work afterwards while recovering and convalescing. Mr Tucker agreed to allow me to go, providing his instructions were followed. He would put my leg in a plaster cast that I could unstrap at night, and replace in the morning. I must have a trained nurse and masseur with me to keep my leg muscle in shape; he also said that I would only be able to put the minimum weight on this foot. Perhaps enough to take a small step into a three-quarter shot, so a double had to be used shooting his back when my character was needed to walk or run. I was to walk on elbow crutches and as little as possible when not filming.

So it was arranged and off we flew to Kenya, I as a cripple on crutches. During some of the shots I occasionally put too much weight on this foot; the pain was then so excruciating that I would fall down. The nurse at once unstrapped my plaster cast, gave me a pain-killing jab, replaced my cast, and we would carry on. Altogether, not the happiest way to make a film in the wilds of Africa.

One incident in Kenya I should mention. My character, against the orders of the white hunter, Victor Mature, had gone off on his own to stalk and shoot a lion. However, the lion decided to stalk my character. The lion was about to spring on me when Victor shot it, and the lion fell dead on top of me. Naturally, this scene was all faked. The dead lion fell on my double, the poor beast having already been shot by a real white hunter the previous evening. I then had to crawl, with assistance, under the lion and replace my double. The lion was beginning to smell somewhat high, and the flies abounded. I now had a scene with Victor, where he tells me what a bloody fool I had been to disobey his orders. All the time, during some lengthy dialogue, I remained under the lion. This scene took half a day to shoot, and the flies had to be cleared off with insecticide before each take, as they do not normally accumulate round a freshly killed animal.

Who really wants to be a film actor? There are times when I think we are certainly underpaid.

I had arranged for Bill Tucker to operate the week after the picture was completed. Nan came with me and installed me in the London Clinic.

CHAPTER XVI

Five Fingers

Bill Tucker performed the suture on my leg successfully. It was not too painful. I was in the clinic for a couple of weeks. When I left, once again in plaster and on crutches, Bill told me that I would probably remain on these crutches for a month or more. But much to Bill's annoyance and disgust, I developed a stitch abscess which set me back for weeks. It was indeed sixteen weeks from the operation before he gave me a clean bill.

I achieved two things during my time of convalescing; as an occupational therapy I learnt to do grospoint. I made a couple of chair-seats. I also wrote a play, *River Breeze*. The story drew a picture of Regatta Week at Henley. Nan and I became rather involved in the Regatta, as she had three nephews who rowed for Shrewsbury. The middle brother, the largest and heaviest of the three boys, was a fine athlete, who on one occasion rowed in the winning four in the Stewards, whilst rowing for the Thames Rowing Club. He was the nicest, kindest, most helpful and polite young man it has ever been my pleasure to meet, and Nan was quite devoted to him.

River Breeze was not a very good play, but several people thought it was very amusing to read, including Binkie, Jack Minster and Kenny More. Binkie was prepared to present it if backing could be found, and Kenny was now in the big money and had a company and was anxious to back the whole production. I fear Kenny lost all his money, and I am sorry that he did, but it really only made a company loss which the Inland Revenue could well afford. Nevertheless, I was very sorry that Kenny had backed a loser, and I think Binkie kept it on a couple of weeks too long hoping, since the audiences laughed, the play would beat the press. But the critics won.

The story was not very original and certainly not in the fashion at that time. The kitchen-sink held sway in the theatre in those days, and drawing-room comedy was old hat. I had a good cast, headed by Phyllis Calvert and Naunton Wayne, who accepted their parts because they amused them. They were both excellent. Naunton with his great charm and twinkling personality was quite expert with his timing and humour, and got more laughs than I had written for him. I played in it myself, persuaded to do so by Binkie and Jack Minster, who directed it, although I had not written the part for myself, and had thought of Bob Coote who was not available. We tried the play out, first in Edinburgh, where we played to packed houses and received good notices, which encouraged us to think we might have a success. We then played Glasgow, where we had a fair press but not quite such good business, and then on to Brighton, where we did quite good business, but the press gave us an inkling of the shape of things to come.

The lady critic started her notice: 'When I saw the programme, before the curtain rose, I read "The action takes place in the garden room of the Denny's house, on the river at Henley". I knew I was going to be bored.'

So bored she determined to be, and bored she proclaimed she was. And I'm afraid the London critics also yawned their way through the evening. I had written a light bit of nonsense, more to amuse myself while convalescing than expecting a production, and was frankly surprised when Binkie, Kenny, Jack Minster, Naunton and Phyllis were so enthusiastic about my effort. I have to say that the audience laughed a lot but the critics did not mention that.

While at Barn Elms in 1956, I appeared in my first television play, *The Letter*, by Somerset Maugham, when for the second time I had the great pleasure of working with Celia Johnson. It was not only a pleasure, but very convenient for both of us, as she lives outside Nettlebed, about five miles farther out from Henley, and we used to take turns in driving to and from rehearsals, as we have done many times since in other productions of television and stage plays.

When living in Barn Elms, we decided that we would like to live in the countryside, if possible, high in the Chilterns near Henley, and finally we found the house we wanted. It wasn't much of a house, but had a marvellous view, the most beautiful hereabouts. There were twenty-two acres of rough shoot and an acre and a half of garden.

Before we moved, we made several alterations, such as building an extra bathroom adjoining our bedroom. Many other improvements were made. Soon as we started our life there, in August 1958, Nan gave me a yellow Labrador bitch puppy, of two and a half months. She was born on midsummer's eve, and with supreme originality was christened Titania, which naturally became abbreviated to Tina. She was the only girl in the world, and, one day, met the only boy.

I worked in several films during 1957 and 1958, of no particular interest. Then in May 1958, Binkie sent me a play by a new author, Peter Shaffer, *Five Finger Exercise*, to be directed by John Gielgud. I read it and was thrilled, not only with the play, but with the part. Adrianne Allen was to play my wife, and two young actors whom I had not previously met, both brilliant, Brian Bedford and Michael Bryant, and a very young, talented actress, Juliet Mills, made up the remainder of the cast.

Five Finger Exercise was a play about a disunited family. My wife considered that she had married beneath her. I was a rather sad, common self-made man, something of a bully who vainly wanted the love of his son but went the wrong way about achieving it and my wife helped to turn him against me. Brian Bedford was the son. Michael Bryant played a German tutor to the teenaged daughter played by Juliet Mills. Juliet's part was the only happy character in the play. I haven't room in this history to tell the story of the play—for any readers interested, all Peter Shaffer's plays are published and well worth reading. Every part was splendidly acted. For myself, I think it was one of the best performances that I have ever given.

Adrianne Allen I had known well for many years. Once, before the war, she played in a sketch I had written for The Green Room Rags. She was excellent. Incidentally I sold the sketch to Vic Oliver. Adrianne had had a distinguished career in London and New York and I rightly thought that she would be a big asset to the production.

We went into rehearsals in June. John Gielgud has the happy knack of getting the best out of his cast, but I should warn any young actor who may be privileged to be directed by him not to mark the stage moves on the script in ink, as at the end of a couple of weeks' rehearsals, each page might well resemble a pattern of tangled knitting, John being a little hazy for some time as to where on the stage the actor should be at any given moment. If you must mark your script, not a practice of mine, use a pencil, have a good large piece of India rubber to hand, and by the dress rehearsal you will know exactly where you are. John's method, of course, takes a lot of the monotony out of rehearsals, each day is an adventure and one is kept on one's toes.

We rehearsed a month for *Five Finger Exercise* and tried out at Cambridge. After the first night it seemed clear that we were in for a success, not that success in Cambridge was a guarantee of a London success. But we were not disappointed. We opened at the Comedy Theatre in July and received similar applause on the opening night and an excellent press next day, also in the Sunday papers. The whole cast received unanimous praise from the critics except from Kenneth Tynan who said that Roland Culver and Adrianne Allen gave Shaftesbury Avenue performances. I don't quite know what Shaftesbury Avenue performances are, but Mr Tynan maintained that they are inferior.

We played to packed houses for fourteen months. Some time before the end of the London run, we heard that the play had been bought for New York, and it seemed probable that we would all be invited to play on Broadway. Adrianne was looking forward very much to this visit to the States; she had played in several successes in New York. She also had an American husband, and many of their mutual friends lived on Manhattan Island. I think she had gone as far as to arrange to stay with one of these friends, so sure was she of the visit.

The three youngsters and myself had signed our contracts to go but not Adrianne, she was not invited, and I knew when I signed that she was not to go. I cannot remember why I knew, but I had the misery of acting with her for several weeks, knowing she was going to get an ugly slap in the face. Neither Binkie nor John had the courage to tell her the news. Had I been in their position I might well have funked it too. Finally, one of them had to tell her, I don't know which. The reason given was that American Equity would not allow more than four of the cast to go if the fifth part could be found from a US resident member of Equity, and as Jessica Tandy was such a resident, and had agreed to play the part, there was nothing that Binkie or John could do about it.

It broke Adrianne's theatrical heart. She went with her husband, Bill Whitney, to live in Switzerland, and has never appeared on the stage again. I don't know that she has ever been to a London theatre since. There's no business like show business.

Several winters ago, Nan and I had a holiday in Marrakesh, where we happened to meet Adrianne and Bill. We played golf together most days, but I don't think the theatre was discussed.

When the four of the *Five Fingers* arrived in New York, we immediately started rehearsing with Jessica Tandy, now married to Hume Cronyn. We rehearsed for three weeks and tried out at the

Dupont Theatre in Wilmington, Delaware—a barn of a place, a hall rather than a theatre, and the acoustics were appalling. After the first night, the management announced that we could not be heard.

Then the producer, not I hasten to add John G the director, sprang rather a surprise on us. He told us that he had summoned a voice coach from New York who would rehearse us the next day and teach us how to breathe! I am aware that I have only one and a half lung power but I had always considered that I had full command of this limitation. The rest of the cast had two whole lungs each and they all believed that they too knew how to breathe. At this time I had been thirty-six years in the theatre, Jessica some several years less. Jessica took this threat of instruction rather on the chin. I confess to thinking it slightly insulting, but nevertheless amusing.

Then we met the fellow, and he turned out to have a broken accent of German origin. I thought it hilarious that he should teach me to speak English. Wonderful things happen in showbiz in the States. No actor should miss a trip.

After Wilmington we did several other towns starting at Boston. Nan did not accompany me originally, too much of a gamble. But come Washington, it seemed clear that we were going to be a success. So I telephoned her to pack her bags and join me in New York. The play opened at the Music Box Theatre a few weeks before Christmas, received a splendid press and at once played to good houses.

All went swimmingly for some months. Vivien Leigh was appearing in *Duel of Angels* with Jack Merivale in the cast. Rex was also there in Anouilh's *The Fighting Cock*. So we had plenty of friends around. Nan and I had a pleasant apartment on West Seventy-Fourth Street, where we entertained. But in May, a dispute between Actors' Equity and the New York Theatre Managers became critical. I cannot say I exactly understood what Equity was demanding. I believe a rise of the minimum salary was one bone of contention. There were several disputes under discussion, but at the end of May no agreement had been reached. Now Equity threatened industrial action. One theatre a night, not to be named more than an hour before curtain-up, would be called out on strike.

On 2nd June, this threat was carried out and the cast of one play instructed by Equity to strike. The particular theatre affected by this action naturally had to return the money for the seats booked for that night, as the audience arrived. Clearly, neither the theatre managers nor the public could be put to this nightly inconvenience, and the following day the managements announced the closure of all New

As Lord Cumnor in *Wives and Daughters* driving through his villages.

'My coronet is at your feet. If you will allow me to raise it I will place it on your brow.'
Barbara Murray as Madame Max Goesler and myself as the Duke of Omnium in the BBC
production of *The Pallisers*.

As the Duke of Omnium in *The Pallisers*.

York theatres until further notice. Equity now maintained that this action constituted a lock-out, and all the actors and actresses engaged must report to their individual stage doors each evening at the half-hour, thus expressing their willingness to appear. They were then required to remain there until the time that the curtain was scheduled to go up.

This unhappy situation lasted ten days, during which time there were several Equity meetings which many of us attended. Rex's play had been closed for some time, but he was still in New York and joined us at these meetings. Afterwards, we would usually gather, that is Vivien, Jessica, Merivale and Rex, and one or two others, at Sardi's for a drink and perhaps supper, or meet at one or the other of our apartments.

That several of Equity's grievances were justified, there is no doubt; certainly the minimum salary needed to be raised. Whether the action they took was the right one, and how many of their demands were met as a result of that action, I don't know. I do know that several plays that had been playing to marginal business, but kept alive by the various managements involved, trying to nurse them along hoping for better houses, never reopened after the lock-out, so that many actors who had been hoping for their plays to run for some weeks or perhaps months longer, found themselves out of work. I am, thank God, no politician, and for me that ten days was no part of showbiz. I sincerely trust that I am never involved in such another stoppage.

One of the plays that never opened again was *Duel of Angels*. Before the stoppage Jack Merivale and Vivien had started living together and this so called lock-out had a bad effect on Vivien. She, poor darling, was a schizophrenic and manic-depressive. Jack was wonderful with her but he didn't have an easy time. However, Vivien was a very courageous woman, when she felt she was going too far off the rails she would voluntarily surrender herself to shock treatment which, I believe, is a very distressing experience. Nevertheless it worked with her.

Five Finger Exercise did reopen after the stoppage, and we ran through the summer until September, when we started on a long tour, visiting very many cities, beginning in Boston. Juliet Mills did not come on this tour with us. Her part was taken over by Pinky Johnson.

Take a pin and stick it in any city on the map of North America from Toronto, then Boston, through the middle west to California, we visited that city on the tour. As on an English tour, we dodged about, north, south, east, west, sometimes we had a night's journey and we would be travelling for twenty hours or more.

We enjoyed a great deal of these tours, particularly Boston, Philadelphia, Toronto and finally Los Angeles, where we met a lot of old friends and stayed two weeks. Once again, I had a couple of games at my old golf club. I also saw my Beverly Hills dentist, whose choppers I yet retain; he was as always most friendly and made me an Honorary Member of the Los Angeles Country Club during my stay. This is the most exclusive club, near Hollywood, with two beautiful golf courses. Needless to say, I took full advantage of this membership. But, by the time we had reached California, I was becoming dreadfully weary of the play, good as it was. I had ceased to enjoy it. I had been playing the part for nearly three years, and I wanted a change.

I had booked a state room on the *Liberté*'s last voyage from New York, at the beginning of April. When, about three weeks before this, the management asked me to do two extra weeks, I couldn't face losing my passage in the ship, and as my contract was at an end, I refused. Well, it gave my understudy a chance, also Jessica's, as she left with me.

Nan and I had a very pleasant voyage home in that splendid ship; we had a delightful state room and of course ate delicious French cooking. Nevertheless, pleasurable as our five days at sea had been , we were very happy to be greeted home by a lovely spring day, with the sun shining brightly on the garden of England, as we sailed up the Channel to Southampton.

The second weekend, after returning home, my sister Iris and her husband visited us. It was then that I learned of her illness while I had been in America, and she was still far from well. As a child, she had always been delicate and suffered from fearful headaches and sickness. It was clearly this failing that finally caught up with her. She died a few months later, miserably ill, in the London Clinic. She was greatly missed by us all, particularly by myself.

CHAPTER XVII

Ivanov and Idleness

During the long frost of 1962/63, I appeared in my first ever Shake-spearian production since the RADA, *Coriolanus*, not on the stage but on the box, the name part played by Robert Hardy. Peter Dews directed. Peter was most helpful to me with the part of Menenius. I enjoyed Menenius very much. I should like to play it in the theatre, but nobody has asked me, which is a pity for in all humbleness and due modesty, I was bloody good.

The production was for the BBC, before their rehearsal rooms at Acton were built, and my chief memory of this engagement was rehearsing in extreme cold and discomfort, in an underheated drill hall at Shepherd's Bush. I never removed a heavy overcoat, hat and woolly scarf during the three weeks of rehearsals. My son Michael chose to be married this winter and we all slid over the ice to the church. He looked splendid and his young bride, Lucinda, enchanting.

During 1961 and 1962 I made several pictures, I think the most notable being *Term of Trial* with Larry Olivier, in the early spring of 1962. We worked in the studios at Bray, near Dublin, and later on location in Paris. It was bitterly cold at that time. I remember that we had to shoot some scenes in the Tuileries Gardens, with the school-girls. The poor children's legs on one occasion were quite blue with the cold and we had to pack it up for the day. Not I think because the producer was particularly concerned for the welfare of the girls, but because blue legs above white socks don't look very good on the screen.

Briefly, the story was about a co-ed school at which both Larry's and my characters were masters. One little bitch wanted to have an affair with Larry's character, he turned her down. Hell hath no fury, etc., so she accused him of trying to seduce her. There was a trial but

Larry was acquitted. Hence the title of the picture. My character was a horse of a different colour. He doubtless would have succumbed to the blandishments of any female, young or old. One scene I have with Larry in a Paris bistro I walk out on him at the invitation of an obvious tart.

That autumn, Nan and I had decided that Wood End was too difficult to run, the garden too large and the rough acreage required too much work to keep the paths in fair order, labour being practically unobtainable. We did have a splendid chap that worked for us three times a week, but it was not enough and we decided to sell the place and moved to a much more manageable house a mile along the ridge, with a completely flat garden and only a quarter of an acre, which after Wood End was considerably easier to manage. We still had a lovely view of the rolling Chilterns, but not comparable to the one that we left.

I was unhappy to leave Wood End, but it really was my own fault that we had to do so, as I never properly pulled my weight in the garden and grounds.

More films in 1964, then back to the theatre in yet another flop, this time a strange one. I was sent a play in which Ralph Richardson was to play the leading part. I was to play his rather unpleasant doctor. An effective part. The play was written by Graham Greene. Naturally, we all hoped for a success, but were disappointed, I particularly as I had never acted with Ralph before and the Haymarket Theatre is my favourite playhouse in London. We only ran six weeks.

In April 1965 I was offered a film starting on location in Cascais in Portugal for six weeks, followed by work in the studio in Rome for a month. This was a very remunerative job and very pleasant. I received sufficient living allowance to permit Nan to accompany me without spending any of my salary. My pal Bob Coote was also in the cast, which was fun, and on days off from shooting we played golf on a very pleasant course. The film was a comedy thriller. I played a doctor who turned out to be the villain. The picture was not exactly a howling success, but we enjoyed making it.

Soon after reaching Rome, I received a letter from my agent with a script of Chekhov's *Ivanov*, which John Gielgud was going to direct and play in, and was asking me whether I would like to play the part of Lebedyev. I read it, and immediately decided that it was for me. A very good part, and I had no doubt the production would succeed. We were to start rehearsals in July. Meanwhile, we had an amusing time in Rome finishing the picture.

My old friend Alan Wilkie flew out and joined us in Rome for a few days, before accompanying Coote and Nan and me on a holiday which we spent in a mutual friend's hotel, near Porto Ercole. I hired a car in Rome for this holiday. Nan and Alan and I were all set to travel. Coote had finished his part and had gone ahead by train a day or two earlier. I was suddenly required at the studio for some extra days' shooting, so Nan and Alan motored off on their own, leaving me to follow by train when I was free. Nan and Alan had an adventurous journey, as after three-quarters of their drive, the roof of the car collapsed, and for the remainder of their trip Alan had the somewhat exhausting job of holding the damn roof up so that it did not rest on their heads. Before our return journey to Rome, I had the ingenious idea of jamming a broom between the floor of the car and the roof, the broom bristles against the roof. This was a success. I can't remember whether the hire firm refunded any money for the inconvenience when we delivered it back to them. I think they paid for the broom!

The part of Lebedyev required me to wear a beard, so I started to grow one on the first day of our holiday. During those two weeks, I looked pretty scruffy. Nan didn't like it, Cootey didn't like it, Alan, I think, was unmoved, but I suspected our friend and host thought my unshaven appearance rather let down the tone of his hotel, and I believe considered it necessary to explain to any new arrivals the reason for my tramp-like appearance.

Arriving back in our country home, of course our first job was to collect Tina, who had been staying with Gladys at Barn Elms. Gladys had also taken care of our black cat, Ellie, whom I have neglected to mention before, which is unkind of me as little El, as she was known, was a charming character. We originally had two kittens, a black Persian, a male, and a smooth-haired animal, a female. These two cats for reasons not too difficult to guess were named Abelard and Heloise. Abelard was a great character. One trick he had was to sit beside the television and try to rub out the actors. Very often I agreed with him.

Unhappily, Abby had to be put down, as Nan found him one day at the side of the road with his front leg severed. Whether he had been hit by a car or caught in a fox snare, we did not know. Whatever the cause, the vet maintained it would be unkind to amputate and try to save him. Just one more animal tragedy.

We started rehearsing for *Ivanov* in July, and opened at the Yvonne Arnaud Theatre in Guildford, and a very happy opening it was. John is a delightful and completely unselfish actor to work with. I had a long, rather charming scene with him in the third act, which I enjoyed immensely. I had several lengthy speeches to which he listened as attentively as I did to his. Listening in the theatre is as important as talking. I think John enjoyed acting with me—I certainly hope so.

After Guildford we played Brighton, then opened for a limited run at the Phoenix Theatre in September. We had been booked to do a Canadian and United States tour in November, before going to New York. We had a successful London season. During the London run I was delighted to receive a charming letter from Bing, saying he had never seen a Chekhov play and did not expect to enjoy it, but his wife had insisted on taking him to see us. He had, he said, thoroughly enjoyed every moment and asked me to congratulate the cast. I pinned his letter to the notice-board. Several of the leading members of the company came to America, except Vivien Leigh replaced Yvonne Mitchell as Anna Petrovna, and Jennifer Hilary took over from Claire Bloom as Sasha, and Jack Merivale played Lvov in place of Richard Pasco. Nearly all the smaller parts were played by American actors and actresses. Happily, Helen Christie, who is great fun to have in a company, came with us in her original part of Babakin.

We arrived in New York in February and had several weeks' rehearsals with the new cast, so John had lots of fun directing the new girls and boys, and leading them round the mulberry bush. But, as always, no one bumped into anyone else on the first night. In March and April we visited Boston, Philadelphia, Toronto and Washington, before opening in New York in May. During the whole tour and the run in New York Vivien was quite relaxed and well, except in one town, I forget which, both she and I arrived with stinking feverish colds, but we were not off from the theatre.

Several amusing incidents occurred on this tour, but it would take up too much space to recount them all. One comedy/drama is perhaps worth a mention. When in Toronto a Canadian friend of the Merivale family, one Rupert Young, volunteered to drive Vivien, John, Nan and myself out to the country on the Sunday, to lunch with friends of his, the Dale Harrises. Jack, who would normally have accompanied us, had to visit a nephew. Mrs Dale Harris, Dodie, is incidentally Leslie Howard's daughter. We had a very pleasant day and on our return to Toronto we all went up to Vivien's apartment for a drink. John left us to put his feet up for an hour in his own apartment, on the same floor opposite Vivien's. He and Vivien had arranged to see the film *The Sound of Music* later that evening. Rupert, Vivien, Nan and I had a drink or two when Rupert asked, 'Has someone dropped a cigarette end? I can smell burning.'

We all looked for a glowing fag-end but no sign of one. However, the smell persisted and became stronger. Rupert said, 'I think there must be an electric fuse somewhere. If you don't mind, Vivien, I'll call reception.' So Rupert picked up the telephone and we heard a dialogue to this effect.

Rupert—'Is that reception?' A pause. 'Well, I'm speaking from Suite 1413 on the fourteenth floor. I think you should send up an electrician. I believe that there is a fuse somewhere, there is a smell of burning.' A pause. 'Oh, really!' Another pause. 'Is it indeed. ' A pause. 'You think not.' Another pause. 'Yes, we will.' Then Rupert hung up and said to us, 'I'm afraid the hotel is on fire, but they say there is nothing to be alarmed about. It's only in the kitchen.'

'The kitchen,' I said, 'but don't flames go upwards?'

Rupert said, 'I had always thought so, but they say it's under control.'

Then we heard a couple of fire-engines draw up. 'Roly,' said Vivien, 'I think you'd better wake John up, don't you?'

'That, ' I said, 'is a thought.'

So out of Vivien's room I went, across the passage—which was becoming somewhat smoky—and knocked on John's door.

In a moment John appeared in vest and shorts. 'What's the matter?' he asked.

'The hotel's on fire, John.'

'Ah,' said John, 'I'm not surprised. I thought I could smell burning. Perhaps I'd better get dressed.'

'Good idea,' I said. 'Suppose you join us in Vivien's rooms when you're ready. We may have to get out.'

'Yes,' said John. 'I suppose so. I'll be with you in a moment.'

I crossed back to Vivien's room, with the smoke in the passage getting denser every moment. I found Nan and the others out on the balcony getting some fresh air and watching the fire-engines below.

Vivien said, 'We thought we might as well freeze to death rather than suffocate.'

We watched the firemen below working away for a moment or two. Then Rupert said, 'Well, I don't think we should freeze, suffocate or burn. I suggest we get out of here and walk to my apartment, only five minutes away.'

About that moment, John appeared and said, 'You can't see more than a yard or two down the passage for the smoke. I really think it would be quite sensible if we made a graceful exit. I don't think I like the idea of being carried down a fire escape on a fireman's back!'

Then we all started for the door. Opening it and looking down the passage, we could not see more than a yard. Nan said, 'Those stone stairs, I think, are an emergency exit. Come on.' With that, she started leading the way down the stairs to be stopped by a fireman who informed her we couldn't get down that way, we must take the elevator. It was certainly nice to know that the elevator was working, but could we find it?

We groped our way through the smoke, coughing and spluttering, most unpleasant, and gained the lift which fortunately arrived quickly on our summons. The smoke in the lift seemed even worse than in the passage. We descended some three floors and stopped. The doors opened and two chaps, who had no intention of losing any of their belongings, started putting suitcases in the lift. One held the doors open while the other put in the luggage. Meanwhile, we were becoming kippered. The men did not apologise for delaying us and I believe thought our protest unreasonable. We finally reached the ground floor and made our way to Rupert's flat.

The hotel was not burnt down. John and Vivien returned to it that night. Nan and I were not staying in the same pub, so we didn't suffer, but John and Vivien retained the smell of smoke in their clothes for some weeks.

We opened in New York in May, for a limited season of two months playing to full houses. I rented a very pleasant apartment from my old friend Renée Gadd. It was most conveniently situated on the seventh floor of an apartment block on West Fifty-Fourth Street, just off Fifth Avenue. So it promised to be a very pleasant stay.

We had been in New York a little over a week and were enjoying ourselves, when one day a hideous telegram arrived from England. Nan was in the bedroom. I opened the cable in the hall. It read: 'Adrian killed West Chiltington love from us all Lesley.'

I was stupefied with horror. Nan's adored nephew. Nan called from the bedroom, 'Who is it, darling?' I couldn't answer. She called again.

I managed to call back, 'A telegram.' Then I walked to the bedroom with this horrible news.

When Nan saw my face, she said, 'What on earth's happened?'

I said 'Darling, the most dreadful news.'

She said, 'Tina's dead.'

'Ah, no,' I said. 'Much worse, Adrian.' I could say no more.

She snatched the telegram from my hand. The next few minutes of Nan's uncontrollable anguish it is impossible to recount. Ultimately, when she had calmed down somewhat, I said, 'Of course you must fly home at once and be with your family.'

Nan said, 'I must know what happened. I must know. I must telephone Lesley.' I said, 'Of course,' and put through the call. Fortunately Lesley, her sister, answered, but the news was even worse than the bare facts of the cable.

Adrian's young brother Jamie was driving Adrian's car with a girl by his side, Adrian sitting behind him with a girl by his side. They had only left their parents' home five minutes previously, when driving round a dangerous curve in a narrow lane they collided with a bus. Adrian was killed instantly with a broken neck, and Jamie was still unconscious in hospital, on the danger list. The two girls were, fortunately, quite unhurt.

Nan flew home to her family next day. Adrian was cremated, and the following Saturday there was a memorial service for him, partly arranged by one of his rowing friends. When the family arrived at the church they were amazed to see it literally packed with young people. Senior boys from Shrewsbury, Old Salopians, Cambridge friends of Adrian's, indeed any young men or girls who had known him or had heard of him. The service had not been publicised, as far as they knew, beyond the family and a few friends. Yet the news must have spread like wildfire to all these young people. Adrian's house-master at Shrewsbury, Mr Michael Hart, gave the address.

When Nan returned to New York life was for a time clouded by this family tragedy, but one cannot mourn indefinitely for the dead, whoever it may be, and Adrian most certainly would not have wished it. In the last month of the run we contrived to enjoy ourselves, giving a couple of parties for the cast in our flat, which were highly successful. 'High,' I fear, being true of several of the younger actors. As host, I was of course sober as a judge; if that is stretching a point, I was never as drunk as a lord.

There is little of interest to mention of the remainder of the New York run, except perhaps that I was nominated for the Tony Award for my performance. But I did not imagine that I would receive this prize. Nicol Williamson was also nominated for his performance as Bill Maitland in *Inadmissible Evidence*, the part being a *tour de force*, he would clearly get the medal. He did.

In July I did a TV commercial in New York for which I was

handsomely paid and, with my savings from *Ivanov*, I was rather loaded with dollars. There was no immediate prospect of any really worthwhile work to return to at home and my accountants advised me that unless some irresistible production turned up it would be best to stay out of England until the following April, and thus avoid paying two taxes on my dollars. The law about this keeps changing and becomes very confusing to a financial nit-wit, so I took my accountant's advice. I decided to take the first part of my exile in Cascais, where I had gained the friendship of a French girl Yvette and her husband, a Dane, who ran a very successful restaurant. They were also excellent golfers.

I flew direct to Portugal and Nan to England. She felt she should visit her family for a time, while her youngest nephew was recovering from his dreadful accident. She sailed to Lisbon three weeks later, bringing her mother, Marjorie, and also our car. Her grandson's death had been a sad blow to Marjorie, and she was grateful and happy that she was able to get away from England for a couple of months.

One quite extraordinary incident occurred in Cascais before Nan arrived. I had frequently praised Yvette for the excellent fish she provided at her restaurant. She said I should go one day and look at the splendid fish market by the harbour where she bought all the fish. I did so and was duly impressed by this large building with a great variety of fish, 'all-alive-o' in their various troughs and compartments. Some of the troughs measured, perhaps, eight feet square with a white marble or composition wall, perhaps two feet high, enclosing the fish. I had finished my exploration of the market and was on my way out when I was accosted by an Englishman, whom I took to be slightly the worse for drink.

'You,' he said, 'are Roland Culver, aren't you?'

This I admitted.

'You don't remember me, I suppose.'

This I also admitted.

Said the chap, 'No, you wouldn't remember me, but I have seen you on the pictures. We were at Skelsmergh together.'

Skelsmergh was the name of my prep school. I said, 'Forgive me for not remembering you, but that must be over fifty-three years ago, and I don't suppose you looked quite the same.'

'No,' he said, 'neither did you. But otherwise you haven't changed. You were just the sort of chap to become an actor, always a bloody show-off at school.'

Oh dear, I thought, I must get away from further chat with this obviously drunken, aggressive ex-schoolboy. I said something to the effect that I had an engagement and he must excuse me. But it wasn't that easy. He stopped me and said, 'We had a fight in the playroom. Do you remember that?' At this point the occasion did come to mind. I remembered a rather nasty little boy with fair curly hair and white eyelashes with whom I had a scrap. Now, however, he had even less hair than I, but retained the white eyelashes and his somewhat mottled complexion looked as though he had suffered several other punches in the face since then, but that may well have been the bottle. I now confessed that I did remember our fight.

'Yes,' he said, 'and the other little sods cheered you on and you broke one of my front teeth. I made your nose bleed.'

'Well, then,' I said, vainly trying to edge away from this embarrassing encounter, 'that made us all square, did it not?' I was by this time standing with my back to one of the fish troughs, but, unpleasant as this encounter was proving, I was not anticipating any physical act on the part of my erstwhile victim. I was wrong.

'What,' he said, 'a bleeding nose to a broken tooth. All square, my arse. But this might square things.' He gave me a push.

The top of the low wall of the trough connected with the back of my knees, and I collapsed, sitting precariously on the edge of the trough. Before I had a chance to recover myself he gave me another shove and I slid gently backwards, among the flapping fish. It was unpleasant and extremely difficult to recover a footing on the floor through the wriggling mass of slimy scales.

I was soon yanked out by a couple of irate Portuguese fishermen who, it seemed, had not observed the reason for my apparent carelessness. My Portuguese was and is limited to 'good-morning', 'good-night', 'thank you', and 'please'. None of these seemed appropriate.

My pugilistic friend obviously made a quick getaway, as there was no sign of him. When I had partially recovered myself and had compensated the fishermen with some escudos for any fish that I might have squashed flatter than normal, I walked back to my rooms, very embarrassed, very smelly, and very cross, and hoping that I might meet him again and break another tooth. But I never did see him again. I bathed and changed my smell, and marvelled that a man could bear a grudge for over fifty-three years.

When Nan and Marjorie arrived we only stayed in Cascais for three weeks. We left in August and motored to the Algarve, where I had rented a house in the country about a mile from Peninna Golf Course, which Henry Cotton had designed. In my story there always seems to be a golf course around! Pure coincidence. The rest of Nan's family joined us there, that is Peter, her brother-in-law, with Lesley and Jamie, the youngest son, still convalescing after his traumatic accident. They all stayed until September when Nan and I moved once more further along the coast to Albufeira, where again I rented a little house in a new estate, about two miles from town. My friend Tam Hugh Williams, had a small house in the centre of the town where he and his wife, Margaret, lived on the top of two floors, while on the ground floor Margaret ran a boutique.

Tam and Margaret had, over the past several years, written a number of successful plays together—much of their work was done in this house. Nan and I spent a lot of time with them on this occasion; we would swim most days. Gladys's daughter, Sally, spent the last two weeks of our stay with us and we all enjoyed a very pleasant time together.

A friend of ours, Peter Montague-Evans, who had been a neighbour in Fawley, now lived in the South of France in his villa at St Jean Cap Ferrat, and had successfully negotiated with some friends of his, who owned a villa at Eze-sur-Mer, to let it to me from 8th October to 15th March 1967. The rent was very reasonable and well within my budget. So on 30th September we set off on our journey to the South of France. Sally accompanied us to Cascais, where we stayed for two days. We then left her at Lisbon airport and set out on our journey through Spain and arrived at St Jean Cap Ferrat on 8th October, there meeting Peter at his home. He escorted us up to our villa at Eze, which proved to be quite charming, about 200 feet above the Petit Corniche with a glorious view of the Mediterranean. Cap Ferrat across the bay to our right. By far the best position on this part of the hill.

So here, for six months, Nan and I idled away our time and thoroughly enjoyed the winter months. I did a bit of painting, but most of it disappointing. On the whole we had good weather, except about three weeks in November when we had torrential rain. These were the rains that were so disastrous to Florence and flooded that city.

In December I received a letter from Tam saying that Peter Bridge had asked him to play the bishop in Shaw's *Getting Married*, to start rehearsals mid-January. But Tam had explained to Peter that he could only play in it for six weeks, as he had arranged to have an operation in April. Peter agreed to give him a six-week contract if he could persuade me to take over the part when he left. In his letter Tam asked if I would be willing to do so. This suited me down to the ground after my months of idleness. I would go straight back to work at the beginning of April. So it was arranged.

We had to leave our villa in March when I found my budget allowed us a visit to Venice and Florence. We left France for Venice on 14th March. There we spent a very pleasant week of sparkling spring sunshine, when the slanting evening rays of light enhanced the beauty of this unique city.

We were not so lucky with the weather in Florence; it overcast and drizzly most of the week with only occasional sunshine. The city had not yet recovered from the dreadful floods of the previous November. Restoration was in progress, but the Ponte Vecchio was still a shambles, and in the lower lying parts of the city the water squelched up through the surface of some of the cobbled streets as one walked along. The flood high-water mark was still to be seen in churches, museums, etc., the level varying from three or four feet to ten, twelve, or fifteen, according to the position of the building in relation to the contours of the city.

We left Florence on 2nd April, to return to St Jean Cap Ferrat, there to stay one night with the Montague-Evans before leaving for home on the Tuesday. Not hurrying through France we arrived at Dieppe on Friday where we boarded the ferry to Newhaven.

CHAPTER XVIII

The Sixth Age

On reaching home our first duty and pleasure, as always, was to collect Tina and Ellie from Barn Elms, where they had both lived during our long absence. Tina was ecstatic at our return and, I regret to say, jumped into our car without so much as a thank you for the kindness and care bestowed on her by Gladys and Gracie.

Gracie, Gladys's sister, I have not previously mentioned in my story, yet we have been close friends with her since our return from California in 1949. She is a darling funny little person who, unhappily, was born stone deaf. She has suffered her long life of silence with great fortitude and humour. She frequently stayed with Nan and me when Gladys had to be away. She was able to communicate satisfactorily by lip-reading and hand deaf and dumb language. Her great pleasure, over the last twenty-seven years, has been watching television. Now the poor darling is gradually going blind. She can scarcely see the TV and can no longer lip-read. Communication is becoming more and more difficult. Such are the unkind afflictions bestowed indiscriminately by providence on some innocent humans. Since Gladys's death, she has lived with and is cared for by Robert Morley and her niece, Joan.

During the last several weeks in France I had been studying the part of the bishop in *Getting Married* and I arrived at my first rehearsal more or less word perfect, and was able to open with about a week's rehearsal. The play had been doing good business and we continued to run for another three months. I thoroughly enjoyed this production. Many old friends were in the cast—Googie Withers, Ian Carmichael, Moira Lister, Raymond Huntley, Esmond Knight, Margaret Rawlings and David Hutchinson. The youngsters I had not met before, but we were all a very happy company.

When *Getting Married* closed I played in a number of TV plays for the remainder of 1967. In December I started rehearsing for *Hay Fever*, playing David Bliss, once again having darling Celia Johnson for my wife. During rehearsals, Celia and I had lunch with Noel at the Ivy one day. He was at this time becoming very frail, and didn't like walking far. Indeed, if I remember rightly, we took a cab about 200 yards from rehearsals, which normally Celia and I would have walked. After lunch at rehearsals, sitting in the stalls with Noel, whom I had known for many years, I said, 'You know, Noel, I'm only playing this part because I have never appeared in one of your plays and because Celia is in it. But it is a rotten part, the worst you have ever written.'

Said Noel, 'Rotten part, Roly? I don't write bad parts, some are better than others and I used to play those.'

This production of *Hay Fever* was produced by Peter Bridge and directed by my old friend Murray MacDonald. We opened at the O'Keefe Centre in Toronto in January 1968. We arrived in Toronto on a Saturday and the thermometer registered twenty degrees of frost. On the Sunday there was a storm of freezing rain and the roads became a sheet of ice. The theatre was only about a quarter of a mile from our hotel but, in spite of the ice, we felt safer carefully walking there than skidding along in a cab. Needless to say, owing to these icy conditions our first night audience was by no means as large as we had hoped, nor for the remainder of our stay did we play to packed houses. But, in the circumstances, we played to fair business. It was a fun cast and we all enjoyed ourselves. But there was one eventuality we had not anticipated and were totally unprepared for. The weather prevented us from flying home on the Sunday, all aircraft were grounded for the day. Another dry Sunday in Canada.

But a hero turned up in the shape of Simon Williams, Tam's son, who was in the cast. On hearing this horrid news, he vanished from the hotel, and on his return produced two bottles of scotch. I know how and where he achieved this welcome miracle, but I think it wiser not to disclose it lest I dry up the source of supply for other Thespians similarly marooned in Canada on the Sabbath day.

We opened in London at the Duke of York's theatre, where we played successfully for several months. Celia is a great cricket fan. She and I have been a couple of times to tests together at Lord's. During the run of *Hay Fever*, at one matinée, there was a madly exciting test being played between England and the West Indies, which Celia and I were listening to on the radio in her dressing-room when not on stage. The last act of *Hay Fever* is very short. It plays about fifteen minutes. I'm ashamed to say that on this occasion we played it at such a speed that it lasted only eleven minutes. Our excuse was that we had to get back to listen to the result of the test.

After *Hay Fever* closed, in 1968, from that July to December 1969, I did nothing but films and television. During that time I played in no less than four films and six television plays. In the films I only played supporting roles, but in the television plays, except for one, I played long leading parts. It is somehow surprising that this chap, then approaching the age of three score years and ten, could learn and assimilate all these words and lines and phrases, when as a boy he didn't learn a damn thing. I'm afraid I have to suppose that when young my school reports were correct—'inattentive and lazy', 'could do much better'.

I don't presume to enumerate the various films and TV plays. They would hardly be interesting reading as nothing particularly amusing or dramatic, as far as I can recall, occurred during the making of any of them.

In December 1969, something very sad and dramatic did occur. On a certain Thursday evening, Nan and I attended the first night of Tam and Maggie Williams's new play, *His, Hers and Theirs*, presented and directed by Murray MacDonald. Tam was playing the leading man, a very long, exacting part. After the play we went round to see him and he was a very sick chap. He said that he had been in great pain all the evening, and at times he thought he would never get through the play. I will not prolong the story of his illness. He was in hospital the next day and died within forty-eight hours.

The play received a fair press and the Sunday papers were kind, but as these papers also announced his death it did not exactly enhance the prospects of the play's success. On the Sunday morning Murray MacDonald telephoned me and asked me if I would be willing to take over Tam's part. The idea horrified me, that I should step into my dead friend's shoes; besides, I said to Murray, I was far too old for the part. Tam himself was stretching it a bit, though five years younger than I was. The character was supposed to be in his middle fifties. Tam was in his middle sixties, I in my seventieth year. Murray would not listen to any of my protests.

'You don't seem like seventy. We will get you a splendid toupee, and you are the only light comedy actor I know who could do the job quickly. Gladys wants you to do it. [Gladys Cooper was in the cast and playing a very amusing part, written for her by Tam.] Maggie wants you and Sam wants you. [Simon Williams, who was also in the cast.] Come along, Roly. Forget your age and help Maggie through her loss and sadness.'

I gave in. Said Murray, 'I'll get a script to you by lunchtime. Rehearsals ten o'clock tomorrow. All right?' I agreed.

'Do you think you can do it in a week, dear boy?' asked Murray.

I said, 'Well, that's a bit of a tall order, but I will try.'

The character is only off the stage for about ten minutes during the whole evening. I did do it in a week. I was not completely word perfect for a day or two after the opening, but I gave a fair performance. Nan suggested that I looked younger if I played the part in my horn-rimmed glasses, as they concealed the enormous bags under my eyes. So I wore my glasses. I was not completely happy wearing them, but I think Nan was right.

Faith Brooke, twenty-two years younger than myself, played opposite me as the girl I was living with, and subsequently was to marry. And she looked every bit of those twenty-two years younger, I fear.

As far as it was possible to enjoy this play in these unhappy circumstances, I did so. Simon was charming and brave, as was his wife Belinda, who played opposite him. And of course there was Gladys. We drove up and down each day from Henley. But the play had had too bad a start, and this old chap, hiding his bags behind glasses, wasn't able to pull it out of the rut. Laughs there were in plenty, and the audiences who came enjoyed themselves. But we couldn't survive and ran, I think, six weeks. Gladys was disappointed. She enjoyed her part and thought we could retrieve the play. Murray was most grateful to me for my efforts and was very sorry that they had been in vain.

The television production of Pinero's *Trelawny of The Wells*, in which I played the Vice-Chancellor, was an engagement I did enjoy. It was beautifully staged and gowned, and expertly directed by Herbert Wise. The whole cast was splendid and we all had a very good time. There was a backlash however to my efforts in this play which was not so pleasant. I will come to it later.

Soon after this I was happy to receive a play from Frith Banbury to act once again with my old friend Coral Browne. I hasten to add by 'old' I mean a friend of long standing! I don't think Coral will ever be old.

The play, *My Darling Daisy*, adapted by Christopher Taylor from the book by Theo Lang, was about Lady Warwick and some letters, or

a letter, to her from Edward VII which she was threatening to publish
in her memoirs. I played Lord Stamfordham and prevented the
publication. The play was a disappointment. I don't think it worth
while to enlarge on the ramifications of the plot here—suffice it, that it
failed. Coral was excellent, was gowned beautifully and looked lovely.
I don't think that there was anything wrong with my performance; the
play just didn't work.

In October 1971 another sadness came to many of us. I returned
home one Sunday to be told by Nan that Gladys, who had been
touring in a revival of *The Chalk Garden*, had been compelled to
abandon it and was in bed at Barn Elms, extremely ill with
pneumonia. Actually, she was dying of lung cancer.

It seemed somehow impossible that this vital, energetic, beautiful
woman, who had appeared to be indestructible, whom I had admired
and loved for so long, was dead.

In April 1972 I was once again in the theatre, married, once more,
to Celia, strangely enough, in a flop and a really unexpected one. The
play was *Me Times Me* by Alan Ayckbourn, who, up to this time, had
never had a failure. The first act was amusing enough, the second
hilarious, but the last, though quite fun to start with, died the death
for the last ten minutes. We opened on try-out in Birmingham. We
worked hard all the week rehearsing, trying to get the last act going,
but to no avail. The tour finished in Brighton, and to everyone's
disappointment never came into a London theatre. I was sad at the
failure of this play for, as must be apparent, I'm always happy to act
with Celia.

My next theatre engagement provided me with the frightening
experience I recently foretold. Phoenix Productions had a musical
version of *Trelawny of the Wells*, with charming music by Julian Slade,
running at the Prince of Wales Theatre, and Max Adrian, who was
playing the Vice-Chancellor, was taken ill. The management having
seen me in the television play begged me to take over the part. They
understood from my manager that I could sing! I have no idea where
my dear manager, Joy Jameson, acquired this knowledge—as far as I
remember, I had never evinced the desire to play in a musical.
However, it so happens that I can sing in tune, quite loudly. I do so in
church on occasions, but whether these sounds emerging from my
vocal chords are pleasurable to anybody but myself, I have never
troubled to consider. I have at times, when singing in the bath, been
politely requested to shut up.

They motored down to our house, arrived with a record of the production, and played on our machine two numbers that I would be required to sing. One was a rather charming little duet with Trelawny, which seemed to present small difficulty, but the other number was a different cup of char. It was a talking-cum-singing affair, with three long verses and a fast rhythm. This I considered would take a lot of learning and rehearsing.

'How soon,' I asked, 'do you want me to take over?' This was on a Saturday afternoon.

They replied, 'Do you think you can get on next Saturday at perhaps the matinée?'

'What, five days' rehearsals?' I choked.

'Well,' they explained, 'you'll have little difficulty with the dialogue as except for cuts it is the same as you have already learnt.'

I pointed out that it was eighteen months since I had played in the television version, and while admitting that doubtless the lines would come back to me without too much difficulty, the general production and stage moves would be entirely different, and need considerable rehearsal. I also protested that, apart from one song I sang, playing Chinaman Ma in a revival of *The Circle of Chalk* at the Arts Theatre Club forty-five years previously, I had never sung on the stage. Nevertheless, they talked me into saying that I would do my best to get on the following week. I rehearsed the action on the Monday with the understudies, and started rehearsing with the conductor in the circle bar with the piano the following day. He was a brilliant young man and somehow contrived to enable me to sing half an octave higher than I thought myself capable of doing. I had no difficulty at all with the little duet, but by the Friday I was still by no means complacent about the long, talking, singing number, and I was to have a dress rehearsal with the principals that afternoon. I was frightened.

My manager, Joy, bless her, doesn't make many mistakes, but on this occasion she let me down somewhat. She did not have it in my contract that I should have a band call, that is a rehearsal with full orchestra, and it hadn't occurred to me that I would not have one. But come that Friday afternoon dress rehearsal, all I had was a piano in the orchestra pit. Now there is a very great difference between singing a number with a piano strumming out the melody and a full orchestra with various instruments entirely disagreeing with each other. Anyway, that is what it seemed like to me on that Saturday matinée when I started off on my long, difficult number, soon after my first few minutes on the stage. To add to my unhappiness, an enormous spotlight that hadn't been manned at my dress rehearsal lit up and followed me around whereever I walked. This I found almost as disconcerting as the orchestration. To be brief, I made a complete bosh of that number on that matinée.

Having been paralysed by the spotlight and orchestration the lyric almost completely departed from my muddled mind, although I retained something of the rhythm. So my rendering of the number went something like this.

No Madam No Madam No Madam No
Obey me obey me or out you go
Your diddle daddle daddle I'm starting to regret
Remember da di da di da you're not married yet
You came here yes you did on approval as a something da di da or
    what you will.
We believed it was essential we should see if your potential would fit
    the la di da you wished to fill
We did expect to meet your diddle daddle incomplete but did not
    expect to meet with a brick wall.
You came into this house on approval but why di da di da and not at
    all.

After some such highly professional rendering of that verse, I was given a slight respite when the chorus sang a dozen bars or so. Meanwhile, I turn my back on Trelawny, walk across the stage, take a silver box from my pocket and have a pinch of snuff.

Of course it is quite unnecessary for an actor to have snuff in a snuff box, he can pretend. But since I am able to take a very small pinch without any ill effects, and being a perfectionist, I had snuff in my box. I opened my box and as a result of my fury at my idiotic performance, and while the chorus were singing out at full blast, I said, 'Oh, fuck,' with great feeling into my snuff box. Which explains why half the contents of my snuff box were scattered over my face and much too much of it up my nose, so that for the remaining two verses I had the further handicap of outbreaks of sneezing. I finally make an exit with my sister, played by Joyce Carey.

When we were off stage I said, 'My God, I made a fair balls up of that.'

'Never mind,' said Joyce. 'Poor Roly, you haven't had enough rehearsals. You'll get it right next time.'

I didn't! But on my third performance I was on the ball, which in the circumstances wasn't bad going. The little duet I succeeded in from the off.

It was an interesting experience. Now at the age of seventy-eight I don't suppose I'll ever be invited to sing again, but should that improbability occur, I will know about band calls; so, I am sure, will Joy.

Very little else of interest occurred in my life at this time except that my darling labrador bitch, Tina, died, a great sadness to both Nan and me.

Soon after bursting into song in *Trelawny* I played in a new farce, *The Bedwinner*, with Jon Pertwee and Linda Baron. We toured for some weeks then opened in London at the Royalty Theatre. However, the play was somewhat of a curate's egg and the audience clearly thought that they had been served up with the bad bits. We did not run very long. So back I went to the box.

Shortly after this I was offered the part of the Duke of Omnium in *The Pallisers*. As a youth, for some strange reason, I had only read one of Trollope's novels, *The Warden*. Just as well perhaps, because I now had a reading treat in store for me at the age of seventy-three. I spent the next six or eight weeks before the production started devouring all Trollope's works. During three of those eight weeks Nan and I were invited by Terry Rattigan to spend a holiday with him in his house in Bermuda. My old friend Harold French was also there with his second wife, Peggy. We all enjoyed a very pleasant time. The garden of the house ended at the edge of the second fairway of a splendid golf course. Surprisingly, however, Trollope kept me away from golf for a great deal of the time.

After this delightful holiday I thoroughly enjoyed my part in *The Pallisers*. No doubt many of my readers will have seen this very expensive and very beautiful production. Now I fear that television viewers will not see many more such elaborate serials on BBC if the Government persist in refusing to raise the TV licence higher than the ludicrous figure of £27. Who do I think I am? A politician? God forbid! But at the moment I am still allowed to express an opinion.

My last appearance in the theatre up to the present time was a rather belated effort at the Bard. I had never performed in a Shakespearian play on the stage since my student days at the RADA. Why? Nobody asked me. Now I played Polonius in the National Theatre production with Albert Finney's Hamlet. During the heatwave of 1976 I also played Agamemnon in *Troilus and Cressida*. This was staged

at the Young Vic, as the Cottesloe where originally we were supposed
to open was not ready. I don't think any of the cast enjoyed this
production very much, the temperature in the theatre was at times
over 100 degrees, concentration was not easy for the actors as we could
see a continual flutter of programmes waved by the audience as fans.
Sometimes a member of the public would pass out and be carried out.
How the actors managed to avoid the indignity I can't think. We must
be made of pretty tough stuff!

When *Hamlet* was transferred to the Olivier Theatre I had an
unfortunate accident. At our first rehearsal the auditorium was in
darkness; the semi-circular stage was black and only lit in the centre.
Thinking to make an exit I walked straight off the stage into the stalls,
a drop of about three feet. Very unpleasant. I received a badly
sprained ankle, which incidentally still pains me in cold weather, but
what maddened me at the time was that I limped through the remainder of the production. As I had not played the character as a dodder-
ing old man, but a virile one, I found this most frustrating.

Well, those were my first and probably my last Shakespearian roles
in the theatre. I enjoyed Polonius until the limp and received a fair
press. Truly one actor friend, a little younger than myself, told me that
my portrayal was not at all his idea of Polonius, in fact it was a bloody
awful rendering. Honestly I did not resent this criticism, indeed I
rather admired his frankness. I should never have the courage to
express such an opinion to another actor however bloody I considered
his performance, and I have thought that about quite a few. Actually I
remember a couple of this chap's characterisations that I thought
stank to heaven.

Since playing Polonius I have been asked many times which Hamlet I liked best and how did Albert Finney's compare with others I
have seen. Friends of mine, to whom I have confided that I am in the
throes of writing an autobiography, maintain that I should write of
my opinion. And now I propose to stick my neck out and hope that I
will not get my head chopped off.

First, I should point out that one gets a very different impression of
an actor's performance when acting with him than watching him from
the front. I am not sure which was the first Hamlet I saw. I remember
John Gielgud many years ago, his first, and he moved me immensely
and he speaks the verse so clearly and beautifully. John Barrymore, I
well remember, and in spite of a trace of an American accent he too
spoke the verse beautifully and gave a most exciting rendering. Also
he was so extraordinarily handsome and such a majestically regal

prince. I recollect that the girl who accompanied me at the theatre that night, one Mary Dawson (I wonder if she is still alive?) was in floods of tears as the curtain fell and didn't snap out of her anguish all through supper.

Larry was a splendid prince and particularly moving in the bedroom scene with Gertrude. But with all due deference to his lordship, to my ears I don't think he spoke the verse as beautifully as John G. Somehow I missed Paul Scofield although I made the gramophone record with him when I played Claudius. I thought his reading—we all read with five days' rehearsals—quite excellent, and as I have collected considerable royalties from the record, clearly the public think so too. Albert Finney's interpretation is, as I explained, more difficult to judge as I was in the production. His was an immensely virile and strong performance but perhaps too strong. I couldn't quite believe that he would have been so irresolute. Nevertheless, it was a very impressive performance. It is difficult for me to comment at all on the bedroom scene as I am dead on the stage at the time lying under a heavy curtain, desperately trying not to move a muscle, sometimes getting cramp, the scene seeming interminable and always hoping either the Queen or Hamlet would cut a chunk of script by accident and relieve me of my discomfort a bit sooner.

Which of these Hamlets, my readers may ask, did I like best? Suppose they look on it as an Agatha Christie mystery story. Not who was the villain but who the hero?

I think I have wriggled out of that rather well.

In the final pages of this book I do not intend to enumerate the various films and TV parts I have played in the last two years. I will just touch on the last one because I played opposite an extremely talented American actress, Julie Harris. She is not only very talented, but a darling person and splendid company. We had many laughs and a lot of fun on the production. A very happy experience. The story of the play I can't tell because it was a kind of whodunit and I must not give the game away.

Unexpectedly I have completed this strange eventful history rather sooner than I expected. I have no doubt that I mewled and puked in my nurse's arms, but that I don't remember. I was certainly a schoolboy, but cannot remember a satchel. Most assuredly I was a lover, but my woeful ballad was made to my mistress's eyelash rather than her eyebrow. For a short time I was a soldier of a kind. I have portrayed a justice on the box—Lord Goddard at the trial of Craig and Bentley.

Many readers will remember this case. It was a cause célèbre. A policeman was shot and killed. Craig was the ringleader carrying a revolver but was only sixteen years old and as a junior could only be committed to prison. Bentley aged eighteen, an adult under the law, was sentenced to death. He was an underdeveloped boy with the mentality of a child of twelve or thirteen. However, on the jury's verdict Goddard had no option but to pronounce the death sentence, but added a strong recommendation to mercy. Maxwell-Fyfe, the then Home Secretary, ignored this recommendation. In spite of national petitions and loud demonstrations of protest Bentley was hung. Craig, after serving his time, never again attempted any criminal activities. He had learned his lesson a hard and sad way.

Lord Goddard was the most interesting character I have ever portrayed on television. The trial was of course *verbatim et literatim* of the original and I had the immense satisfaction, soon after the production appeared on the screen, of receiving a most charming congratulatory letter from Goddard's daughter, Lady Sachs, in which she thanked me for my accurate and honest portrayal of her father and my understanding and sympathy. She also wished me to know that her sisters joined her in this appreciation. During my long career I have had many erudite praiseful letters from the public for various performances and they have always been most welcome. But this letter was, I think, unique.

Goddard seems to have delayed me somewhat in the completion of this history.

At this time I do not feel like a slippered pantaloon, neither I hope do I look like one. Nor in the last stage of all when I reach it do I believe that I will pipe and whistle in my sound, as each year my voice seems to become pitched in a slightly lower key. Indeed, when in church I now find difficulty singing the hymns other than an octave lower than most of the congregation. Occasionally, if tempted to achieve 'Abide with me' in the higher register, heads are apt to turn in my direction clearly expressing the hope that I won't abide with them much longer. Embarrassed I drop my voice an octave.

Rather like some after-dinner speakers I have heard, I seem unable to stop talking; when it is clear, or should be, that many diners are becoming restless and wish to leave the table to relieve themselves of much wine and other beverages they have consumed during the evening.

But in this January of 1979, with the world torn by political disunity, religious bigotry and filled with hate, envy, jealousy and discontent, I found difficulty in judging whether to finish this book on a note of despair and sadness or hope and gladness. Should I return to church and sing 'Change and decay in all around I see, Oh thou who changest not, abide with me'?

On the other hand, I look out of my window this bright frosty morning at the rolling Chiltern Hills, just now covered in a blanket of snow, a blue sky above and the trees displacing branches of sparkling silver lace lit by the bright sunlight, whilst various birds, tits of all kinds, blue, coal, long-tailed and great, with robins, blackbirds and thrushes all gratefully gorging themselves on the special food we put out for them.

It all looks very lovely and one is more inclined to sing:

All things bright and beautiful
All creatures great and small
All things wise and wonderful
The Lord God made them all.

Perhaps He did. Mother believed so. It would be very comforting to have her faith.

Index